IMAGES
of America

# SALINA

## 1858–2008

The Salina Military Band entertained the community for over 12 years under the leadership of Walter H. Packard. The group played its first concert on May 6, 1896, to raise funds for new uniforms. Four years later, after a long debate, the city agreed to allow a $15 a month appropriation to help pay for additional uniforms. Shown here is William C. Alman with bass drum and cymbals looking smart in his full dress attire.

*On the cover*: This photograph of downtown Salina shows a rare angle of Santa Fe and Iron Avenues looking southeast. The numerous horse-drawn vehicles and no automobile in sight suggest this busy day was sometime in the early 1900s. Shoppers might eat at the Elite Café, one of 15 restaurants available, or visit George Caldwell's barbershop. The large building on the corner held many businesses: attorney and physician practices, a novelty company, the Yocker sisters' dressmakers, and several insurance and real estate offices. (Courtesy of the Salina Public Library.)

IMAGES
*of America*

# SALINA
## 1858–2008

The Salina History Book Committee

ARCADIA
PUBLISHING

Published by Arcadia Publishing
Charleston, South Carolina


Library of Congress Catalog Card Number: 2008927004

For all general information contact Arcadia Publishing at:
Telephone 843-853-2070
Fax 843-853-0044
E-mail sales@arcadiapublishing.com
For customer service and orders:
Toll-Free 1-888-313-2665

Visit us on the Internet at www.arcadiapublishing.com

Young people pose playfully during a leisurely Sunday afternoon in Oakdale Park. In 1881, John and Rosine Geis sold about 45 acres to Saline County for $5,500. For many years the county used the property for its fairs, with an exhibit hall, stock barns, and a racetrack. The park held the popular chautauqua programs during the early 1900s. In 1922, under a 20-year lease, the city took over the care and development of the park.

# CONTENTS

# ACKNOWLEDGMENTS

The Campbell Room of Kansas Research and its collections exist because early individuals recognized the value of documenting the history of Salina and Saline County. Prior to 1900, Alexander M. Campbell Jr., the son of a town founder, began collecting and preserving manuscripts, photographs, and ephemera pertaining to this region. Other stewards of local history followed in his footsteps—Effie Davis Campbell, Sherman Ripley, Ida Cooley, Frank Langshaw, and Mary Crowther—and down through the years the Salina Public Library has supported their endeavors. The work of other town historians aided our research efforts as well. Thanks go to Ruby Bramwell Phillips, James Geisendorf, and Mary Douglass.

To put together a photographic history of a place requires cooperative efforts from several sources. The history book committee owes a debt of gratitude for help received from staff members at the Salina Public Library. Special thanks go to Trent Rose and Nick Berezovsky for their time and patience in handling the scanning and technical logistics for the project. Also, we appreciate the encouragement of the Salina Friends of the Library board who agreed to support this project.

The committee would like to thank our editor at Arcadia Publishing, Ted Gerstle, for his guidance through the process of assembling this pictorial. Also, thanks to those who loaned images for consideration or use and granted permission to use them in the book: Al Mattson, Eve Boyle, Donna Moreau, Audrey Peterson, Salina Airport Authority, Salina Community Theatre, Salina Arts and Humanities, Smoky Hill Museum, Smoky Valley Genealogical Society, the Land Institute, the Salina Human Relations Department, Kansas State University–Salina, Kansas Wesleyan, USD 305 School District, and the Salina Journal.

Unless otherwise noted, the majority of the photographs come from the Kansas Collection and the Dale Weis Collection at the Salina Public Library or the Kansas State Historical Society.

The project team consisted of Lori Berezovsky, community outreach coordinator, Salina Public Library; Dorothy Boyle, former registrar, Smoky Hill Museum; Cloie Brevik, researcher, Smoky Valley Genealogical Society; and Judy Lilly, Kansas librarian, Campbell Room, Salina Public Library.

# INTRODUCTION

When Salina was established in 1858, it became part of the nation's great expansion effort that was designed to spread people across the country from coast to coast. Six years earlier Kansas Territory had been carved from the unsettled region west of Missouri, and a number of counties were laid out and given names. But the surveying had stopped at the Sixth Principal Meridian (the Dickinson County line), which meant that the three young men who selected the Salina town site traveled beyond survey lines to drive their stakes beside the Smoky Hill River in north-central Kansas. William A. Phillips, Alexander M. Campbell, and James Muir, all Scottish born, believed the location to be ideal for agricultural pursuits and as a hub of future development. The three men plus the other two members of the town company, Alexander Spilman and David Phillips, felt justified in their expectation that other settlers and entrepreneurs would follow them and that a town would soon grow and thrive.

Although the coming years would prove the Salina town founders correct in their projections that Salina was advantageously situated, the outbreak of the Civil War in April 1861 kept the little settlement frozen in time for the duration of that conflict. Those who remained to hold the town's place in history lived a frontier lifestyle complete with hard times, thrilling sights and sounds, and a few dangers thrown in.

Their unique experiences would never be exactly replicated once the westward flow of "civilization" had resumed. During these years, Salina inhabitants interacted peacefully with Native American tribes, predominantly the Kansa, who lived in their traditional campgrounds during hunting seasons and traded at local stores. Settlers learned the trick of using buffalo brains to soften animal hides for robes and clothing, while Native American women learned that bars of soap could also accomplish the same desired result. Twice a year herds of buffalo thundered along their migratory paths west of the small village on their way south for the winter and back again in the spring. The only conflict that bore any connection with the war raging elsewhere between the states was the guerilla raid that erupted early one morning in September 1862. The group of thieves demanded weapons, horses, and mules purportedly for the Confederacy but more likely for their personal benefit. The ruffians rounded up all the local men in a surprisingly congenial manner and kept them under guard while carrying out a search of the premises for their loot. No one was hurt that day, but to a frontier community in the 1860s, loss of their means to hunt, travel, and protect themselves created noticeable hardship.

As the Civil War ended in 1865, the original inhabitants who had fought for the Union returned, while other veterans and their families from the east, as well as European immigrants, gradually moved west to take up land or start a business. Town leaders worked hard to entice the Kansas Pacific Railway to come through Salina on its way to Denver. When track was completed as far as Salina in 1867 and the first engine chugged into town, the entire community turned out for the event.

Salina has been celebrating milestones now for 150 years, and as the city changes with the times it still maintains many of the goals and values of the original families who chose to make the Kansas prairie their home.

In 1870, Salina became a city of the third class, with Charles H. Martin inaugurated as the first mayor. Energies focused on commercial development and physical improvements to the city; however, losing its frontier appearance and sensibilities was a gradual process through that decade.

During the 1880s, railroad expansion and a building boom developed momentum and laid groundwork for traditions that continue today. Commercial businesses—dry goods, groceries, banks, hardware stores, and furniture stores—opened for business in two-story brick buildings with plate glass windows. A joint stock company made up of local people financed the Salina Opera House, a three-story, brick edifice that graced the southeast corner of Seventh Street and Iron Avenue, and introduced the city to a long-standing participation in cultural activities. Schools were built to accommodate the influx of African Americans who migrated out of the South.

As the years rolled into the 20th century, Salina entered into a prosperous era that lasted for nearly three decades. H. D. Lee was now well established with his thriving wholesale mercantile business that would one day develop into the famous Lee Jeans franchise. The nation's thirst for mass-produced goods proved a boon for the railroads, wholesale distributors, and traveling salesmen. The milling industry, as well as lumber businesses, remained strong. Employment was available for laborers, and in the early 1920s, many families from Mexico moved into Salina to work for the railroad.

Even America's entry into the Great War in 1917 and the influenza pandemic in 1918 did not entirely dampen the optimism that prevailed during this time. But dark days loomed ahead as the community, along with the nation, plunged into first a 10-year Depression and then a second world war. Ironically, World War II brought the Smoky Hill Army Airfield to Saline County in 1942, and in doing so established a positive connection between the community and the military that lasted for 30 years, culminating in a Waiting Wives program during the Vietnam War.

In 1958, Salina residents celebrated the 100th birthday of their city with numerous activities that included a parade and a pageant called Wagons to Wings. Fifty years have passed since that celebration year, and much has transpired within the boundaries of the town. In 1989, Salina was named an All-America City. The legacies of these recently past decades can be found in the city's sound businesses and industries, its healthy schools and churches, its excellent cultural opportunities, its strong civic leaders, and a diverse population. As in the previous 150 years, Salina remains a crossroads of the nation.

# One

# FRONTIER YEARS
## 1858–1879

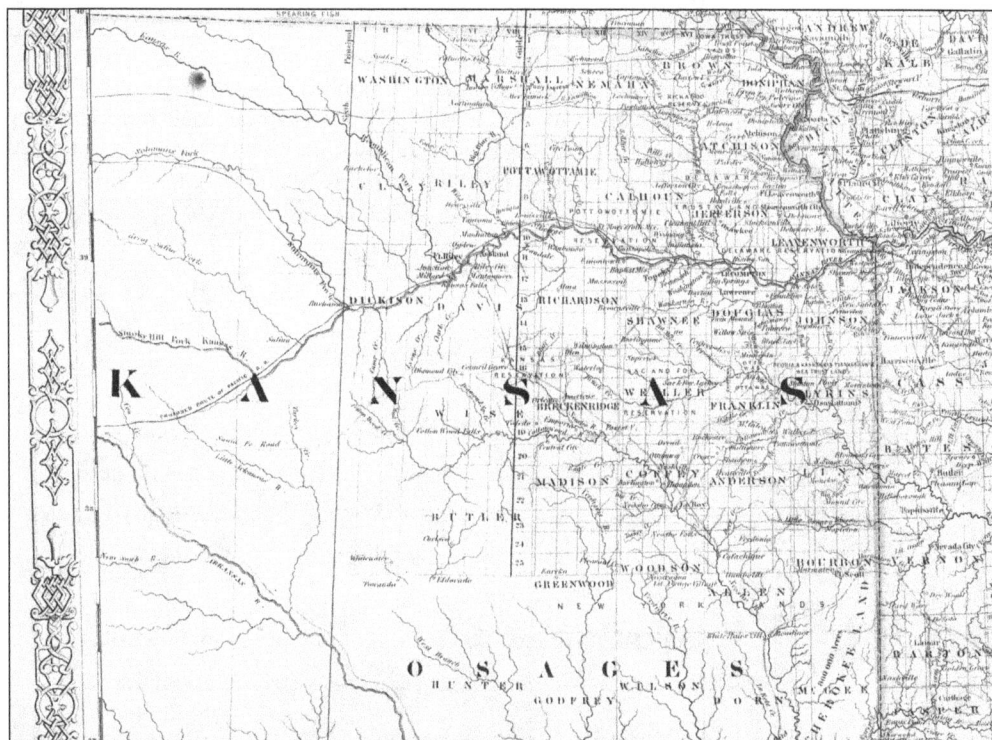

This 1859 map of Kansas Territory shows Salina situated beyond the Sixth Principal Meridian, a north–south survey line that at that time was also the western boundary for Kansas counties. Salina was the region's frontier outpost and served as a supply stop for military troops, hunters, and gold seekers using the "dry route" to the Rocky Mountains. When the Civil War began in 1861, many of the men left to serve in the Union army. Those left behind struggled to secure the town's place in history.

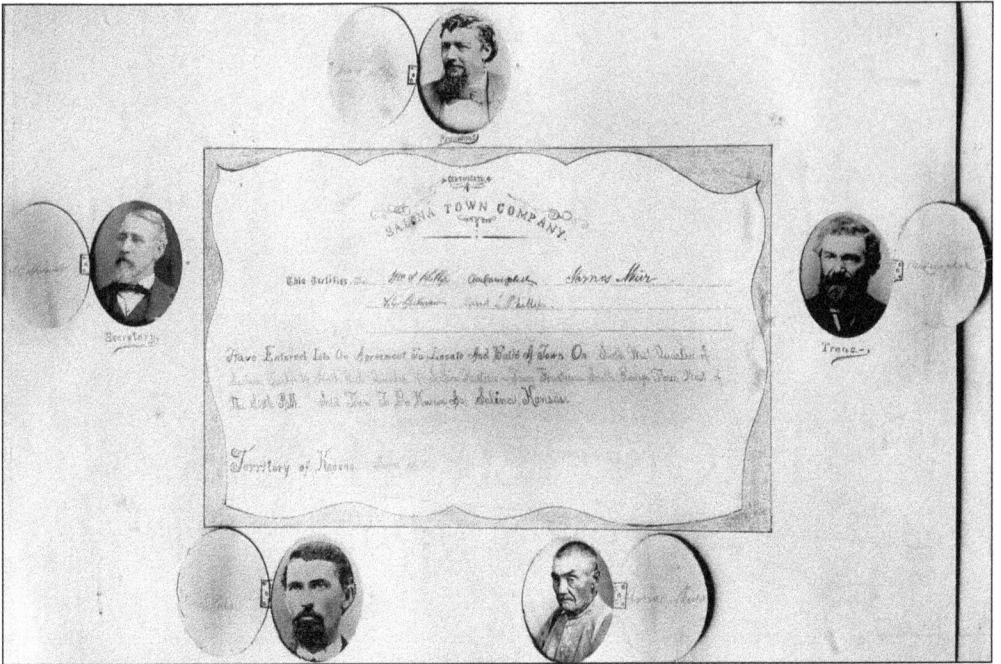

In 1858, five men met in Lawrence to finalize plans for a town in "western Kansas Territory." Those men, shown clockwise, are William A. Phillips, Alexander M. Campbell, James Muir, David L. Phillips, and Alexander C. Spilman. All but Spilman were Scottish born, and all but Muir were related by blood or marriage. Early in 1858, William Phillips, Campbell, and Muir walked west and selected 320 acres near a bend in the Smoky Hill River, some 180 miles from the Missouri River.

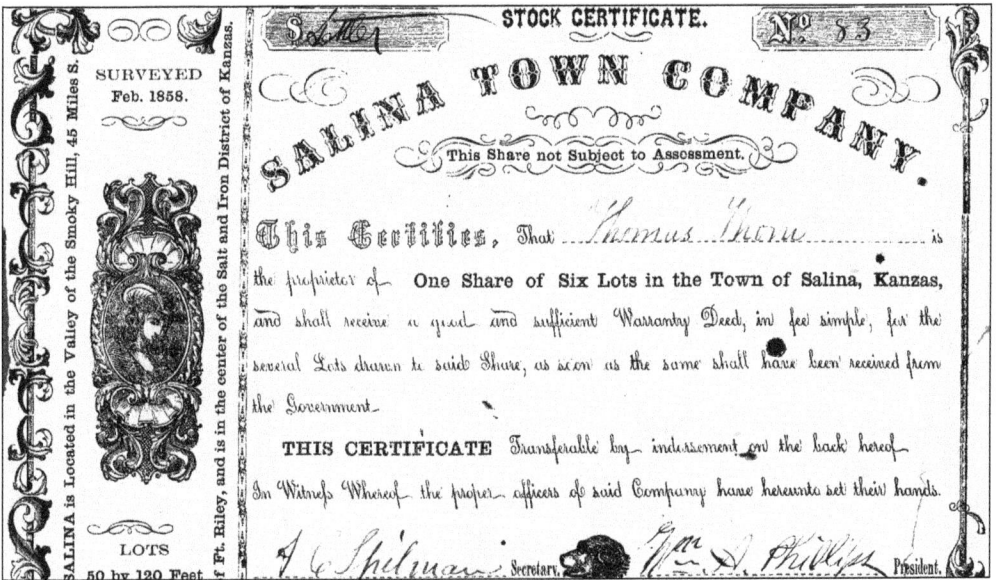

In 1861, buffalo hunter Tom Thorne received one share of town stock entitling him to six lots. After trading one lot to B. F. Robinson, he sold the rest of his share to Luke Parsons for $36.35. Thorne was a colorful character who maintained a log house called "the Den," where frontiersmen enjoyed refreshment and lodging. In the summer of 1864, a band of Cheyenne surprised Thorne in his camp on Plum Creek and killed him.

10

Alexander Campbell, a town company member, and Christina Phillips were the first Salina couple to marry, on November 6, 1858. On that morning the couple and brother David Phillips set out in a covered wagon with supplies and a tent to find an official to marry them. A district judge in Riley City performed the ceremony, and the newlyweds enjoyed a "fine wedding supper" by campfire on the prairie.

Within months of Salina's founding, the first log dwelling went up on the southwest corner of Iron Avenue and Fifth Street. James Muir and Alexander Campbell built a dogtrot cabin with two separate rooms on the first floor and a breezeway in the middle. It also had a loft or second floor for sleeping quarters. Later the middle area was walled into a room. The cabin served as living quarters, a trading post, and a primitive hotel.

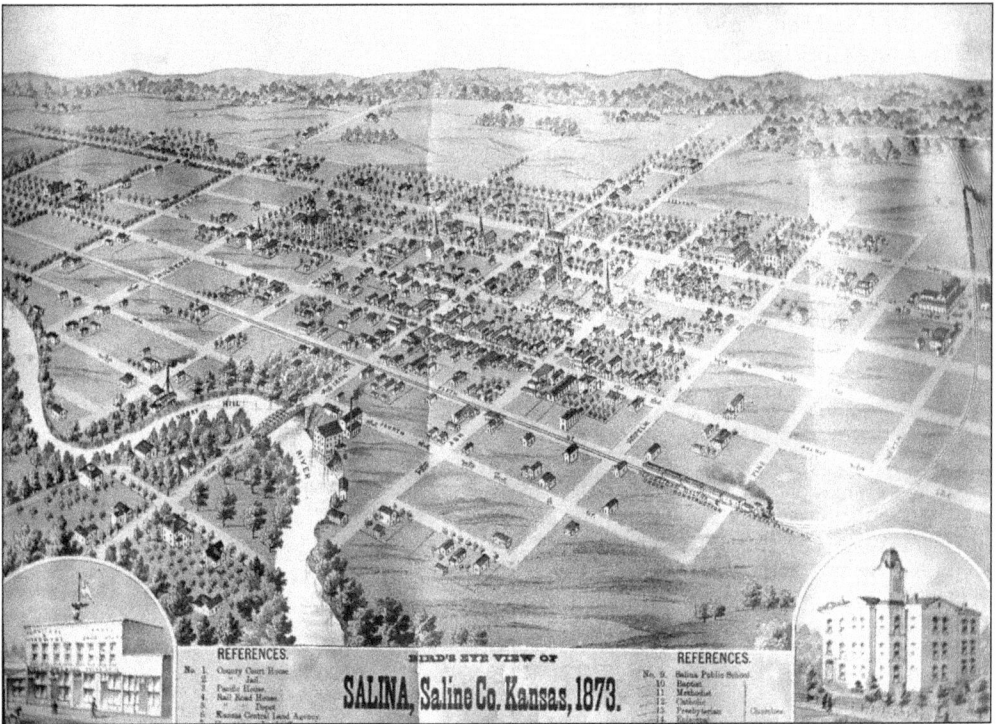

This panoramic bird's-eye view of Salina, done in 1873 by artist/photographer L. H. Mallit, is a fairly accurate representation of how the town had grown in the 15 years since its founding. Visible is the Western Star Mill along the river, the street grid, seven churches, a court house, a three-story school building, a land office, railroad lines, a depot, Pacific House hotel and restaurant, and a jail, as well as the business and residential areas.

The Smoky Hill River was an important partner to the founding of Salina. It provided water for drinking, cooking, washing, bathing, and for the gristmill and sawmill, as well as for flour milling that eventually became Salina's major industry. Shown here is the dam put in by an early mill company near North Street. Early millers were Bernhardt Blau, Ritters and Underwood, Berredell Gower, Eberhardts, and Sudendorfs.

Luke Parsons rode with the radical abolitionist John Brown during Bleeding Kansas days in the 1850s. Born in Massachusetts, young Parsons took part in skirmishes between Free State and pro-slavery factions. Rather than joining the tragic Harpers Ferry raid, Parsons remained in Kansas and in 1860 settled in the new frontier town of Salina, later joining the Union army. He also served as the first Saline County sheriff. (Photograph by F. O. Magerkurth.)

While covered wagons wait at the intersection of Santa Fe and Iron Avenues, settlers passing through town replenish supplies at Ober, Hageman, and Whittredge's general store, the native stone building on the southwest corner. On the northwest corner is a two-story cottonwood frame hotel built by William A. Phillips in 1866. It remained a hotel for several years, but in this picture, dated 1879, it houses a saloon owned by Willis Kesler. The saloon burned in 1880.

13

Early on September 17, 1862, Carl Tressin, a Prussian immigrant, labored in his hardware store as a band of Confederate guerillas rode into town, corralled the men in the street, and confiscated all weapons and horses. Tressin lost the guns he owned plus those brought in for repair. This building stood at the corner of Santa Fe Avenue and Ash Street and typically served dual purposes. St. John's Lutheran Church held its original communion service here on May 11, 1873.

The Morrisons came as an extended family from Illinois on the heels of the original settlers. Two brothers and wives, Whitfield and Mary (McCullough) and Andrew and Nancy (Beaty), along with their families, arrived in 1860 to find a primitive existence. The families helped establish the First Presbyterian Church. Andrew often served as an itinerate supply preacher. Here Andrew's son Hugh and his wife Rebecca (Ewing) pose with their children in a coveted "likeness."

This view of 1875 Salina, taken by photographers Strong and Boyles, shows the railroad tracks running along the north edge of town. The Union Pacific, Eastern Division, reached Salina from the east on April 29, 1867. The railroad remained a major employer in the community for over 100 years. Note the building on the far right. Mary Ann "Mother" Bickerdyke ran this railroad hotel from 1867 to 1869.

This home, reportedly built about 1867 for Ransom and Nancy Calkin, seems stylish for the times, but family tradition suggests Ransom had money from the sale of a sailboat fleet in New York. The couple and their son Royal arrived in Kansas Territory in 1854 and moved west to Salina about 1860. Located at the corner of Lincoln Avenue and North Eighth Street, the house's west wing was to be used as a courthouse. Ransom served as the county's first treasurer.

August Bondi came to America with his parents in 1848 after fleeing oppression in his native Austria. Troubled by the practice of slavery, he ventured into Kansas Territory in 1855 where he fell in with abolitionist John Brown and later rode briefly with Jim Lane, a radical Free State leader. Following the Civil War, Bondi and his wife Henrietta (Einstein) moved to Salina, where they raised a family of 10 children and were part of a small Jewish community.

The Saline County courthouse, built at a cost of $25,000, sat at the southwest corner of Ninth and Elm Streets. The first floor held offices, and the second was a courtroom initially also used for public entertainment. However, the county commissioners soon disallowed dances and parties and decreed the hall could be rented only for lectures that were beneficial to the public. The building served the community from 1871 to 1911.

This view of Ninth Street looking south from West Elm Street was taken in the mid-1870s. The buildings identified by numbers are as follows: courthouse (1), Pacific House (2), Ninth Street (3), Old Central school (4), Presbyterian church (5), Episcopal church (6), Methodist church (7), Baptist church (8), Elm Street (9), and Eighth Street (10). The Pacific House was a hotel and restaurant owned and operated by Catherine E. Jeffries and J. M. Postlewait.

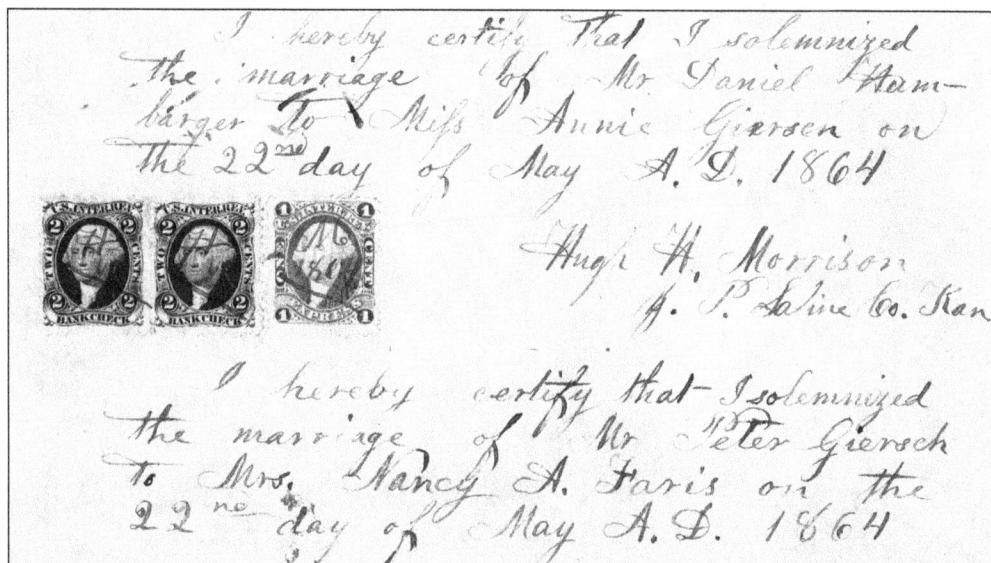

This handwritten document legalized the bond of marriage between two couples: Annie Giersch and Daniel Humbarger, and Peter Giersch and Nancy A. Faris, both on May 22, 1864. Very possibly this was a double wedding officiated by Hugh H. Morrison, justice of the peace. Revenue stamps indicate the necessary fees had been paid. Both the large Giersch and Humbarger families arrived before 1860 and settled in Saline County. (Courtesy of Smoky Valley Genealogical Society.)

This building, erected in 1874, loomed three stories above the landscape and accommodated elementary school children in the city. The brick schoolhouse served for 46 years and came to be called "Old Central." When the third floor was finished, high school students took a course of study, and the first class graduated in June 1878. Two students, Maggie Rash and Arthur Day, made up the entire graduating class. Old Central was demolished in 1922 after the Roosevelt and Lincoln buildings were completed.

The young schoolgirls in pantaloons and boots depict an austere frontier lifestyle in this 1869 photograph made from a tintype original. The chums attended classes in a frame two-story structure with L. O. Wight or Sallie Conant Bean as their teacher. From left to right, the girls are (first row) Lettie Hanna, Belinda Bittenau, Mary Campbell, and Mary Gaylord; (second row) Molly Schutz, Lillie Milaus, Minnie Naismith, Flora Richardson, and Rosa Werry.

Anderson and May Hine were among the stream of nonwhite settlers that poured into Kansas during the latter 1870s. The couple and their children came to the "Land of Milk and Honey," as Kansas was known, from Florence, Alabama, and did well in their new home. Anderson opened a boot and shoemaker shop on North Santa Fe Avenue, advertising his expertise in Salina's first city directory of 1879–1880. Later he had a grocery business. Besides caring for seven children, Mary was a nurse and midwife in the community for 40 years. Their daughter Lulu and neighbor Narcissa DePriest were the first minority students to graduate from Salina High School in 1883. Youngest daughter Clara taught at Haskell Institute in Lawrence for 26 years. The family listed their mixed heritage as Cherokee, West Indian, French, and Irish. (Courtesy of the Smoky Hill Museum.)

STORE
THEN A
SALOON

PLANTERS
STATE
BANK

Boardwalks and saloons were part of Salina's downtown scene, especially before the 1880 prohibition law. One colorful story involves the James-Younger Gang. To the back of this saloon (now the location of 109 North Santa Fe Avenue) was a "garret chamber," reached by back stairs and containing gambling tables and a bed. One night, mysterious visitors took up residence in the chamber for three days and nights. Rumor was that the James boys were laying low after the Northfield, Minnesota, robbery.

R. H. Gardner assembled a variety of men and boys for his photograph in front of James T. Wells's harness shop located at 110 West Iron Avenue. Merchandise for sale included saddles, hames, and straw ticks. Gardner captures the rough ambiance of the town as it was in the latter 1870s. Overhead, Dr. J. W. Daily ran his medical practice, a traditional location for doctors, dentists, insurance agents, attorneys, and other professionals well into the 1900s.

# *Two*

# GROWING GRACEFULLY
## 1880–1899

By 1884, Salina showed signs of business and residential growth. This is a bird's-eye view of Eighth Street looking north from the top of Central School. Central School was located between Seventh and Eighth Street, and Mulberry and Walnut Streets from 1874 to 1922.

Friends gather in the Gemmill family sitting room, in the late 1800s. R. J. and Helen Addison Gemmill moved to Salina in 1884 with a group of Scots from Sparta, Illinois. Daughters Katherine and Jessie, commonly called the Gemmill girls, were longtime schoolteachers in Salina. The Gemmill girls were also known as "Brown Gemmill" and "Blue Gemmill" because of their favorite clothing colors.

Mark B. Palmer, proprietor of the Palmer Opera House Pharmacy, resided in this large home at 222 South Eighth Street, shown here around 1900. The house is still standing, but the roof has been altered. The pharmacy business was on the ground floor of the Salina Opera House at the corner of Iron Avenue and Seventh Street, a three-story building erected in 1877. It was torn down to make way for the United Life Building.

After a brilliant career in the army, Capt. John H. Prescott moved to Salina in 1866. Prescott and his wife Mary pose with their children Henry Lee, Fred Clark, Maude, Margaret, and others who are unidentified. John became Salina's first judge and was state senator from 1866 to 1872. A farmer and landowner as well, he promoted the welfare of the city, being liberal with his means and influence. John did much to secure the location and establishment of Kansas Wesleyan University and St. John's Military School.

The Victorian Italian villa–style, 15-room home was built at 211 West Prescott Avenue for Judge John H. Prescott in 1884. Valin and Johnson were listed as the architect and builder of the home, which was added to the National Register of Historic Places in 1976. Salina's Prescott Avenue is named for the judge, who was a veteran of the Civil War.

A. M. Claflin is shown at the right of the doorway of his grocery store in 1875, at 201 North Seventh Street. The photograph below shows the Claflin family parlor in the living quarters above the grocery store. When downtown districts were built in the 1880s, professional offices occupied much of the upstairs space. A century later Salina has become a model for loft-space development as these upstairs spaces are reclaimed for living quarters.

Ed Lotz is listed as the 1897 proprietor of this wholesale and retail business at 110 and 112 North Fifth Street. Lotz was the only seed dealership in Salina at the time.

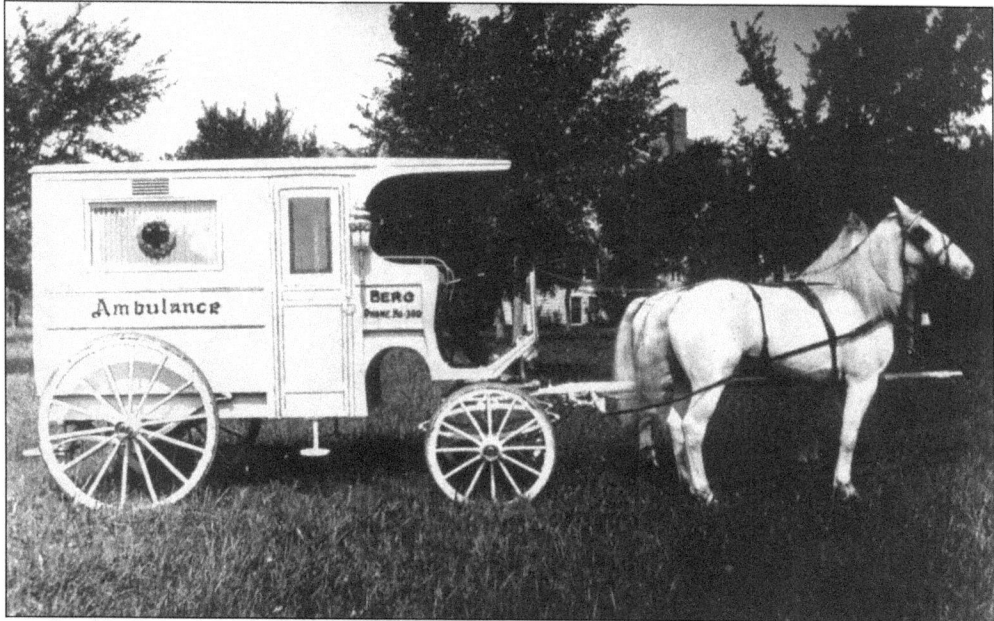

This horse-drawn ambulance is representative of the Berg family undertaking business established in Salina in 1874. Guy Ryan joined the Berg staff in 1909, leading to the longtime locally owned and family-operated Ryan Mortuary business. Operating a combined furniture store and undertaking business was common in the 18th and 19th centuries. Salina Undertakers also offered ambulance service as late as 1966.

Benjamin A. Litowich emigrated from Poland in 1869 and moved to Salina in 1871 to build his future in business. After separate business ventures, Rothchild Brothers and Litowich joined in 1896 to establish the Salina Mercantile Company. A longtime fixture in the community at 104 and 106 North Santa Fe Avenue, "the Merc," as shoppers knew it, closed in 1969.

Benjamin A. Litowich married Juliette Rothchild in 1897. This photograph shows Bernhardt, Juliette, Caroline, Benjamin, Herbert, and Helen Litowich, and an unidentified young lady on the right. The family lived at 683 South Santa Fe Avenue from 1921 to 1958. Son Herbert and daughter Caroline, who was also an author and journalist, joined in the family mercantile business. Son Bernhardt Israel became a Salina attorney, and daughter Helen taught school in Salina for many years.

Henry David (H. D.) Lee is pictured with salesmen N. F. Schwartz, Charles L. Schwartz, Ward L. Harris, W. S. Wakefield, David Arnold, Charles Hessler, L. N. Crain, and L. C. Staples. Lee (1849–1928) came to Salina from Ohio in 1889. He founded the Lee Mercantile Company, which soon became the major food distributor between Kansas City and Denver. A Lee mercantile logo became the inspiration in 2007 to promote the Lee District in downtown Salina.

This Queen Anne–style home was built in 1888 by C. G. Wilmarth for William and Isabelle Flanders. Later, for several years, this was the residence of entrepreneur H. D. Lee, whose businesses included the Lee Jeans factory. The property at 220 South Seventh Street was placed on the National Register of Historic Places in 1987. Nowadays Ron and Cindy Roets live in the home and operate Partridge in a Pear Tree, a gift shop, on the first floor.

Volunteer firefighters stand alongside a horse-drawn chemical wagon in 1887. City council member Tom Quinn became known as the "daddy" of the paid fire department, which began in 1909.

The electric light and power plant was located between Pine and North Streets, east of Santa Fe Avenue, in the 1880s. Power was used earlier in the milling business, but Salina did not experience electric lights until 1887. Salina did not build its own power-generating plant as most cities did, but depended on private entrepreneurs to provide the service. Sources changed over the years, and Westar Energy currently is the provider.

The Salina Hospital and training school for nurses was started and operated by a group of Salina physicians in 1905 in a wood frame house at the corner of South Ninth and Frost Streets. When larger facilities were needed a few years later, St. Barnabas Hospital was built on the grounds of St. John's Military School.

F. A. Loomis,    140 S. Santa Fe.    SALINA,
. . KANSAS

The First Methodist Church in Salina was organized in 1863 with 20 members meeting in a small wooden church building. The brick edifice shown in the photograph was erected at 122 North Eighth Street with the first service being held on Christmas Day 1872. The steeple fell in the storm of 1903 and never was replaced. This building was replaced in 1917 at the same address.

Kansas Wesleyan University, Salina, Kans.

The main building, later renamed Lockwood Hall, was the first building on campus when the Methodist-affiliated Kansas Wesleyan University was founded in 1886. Lockwood Hall was moved southwest in 1921 and demolished in 1929. Pioneer Hall was completed as the main building in 1930. The 28-acre campus became the center of the city as Salina grew up around the college. A $6 million student activities center built around Muir Gym on the northeast corner of campus at Claflin and Fourth Streets is nearing completion in 2008.

Sacred Heart School,
Salina, Kansas.

By 1902, the entire 400 block on the north side of West Iron Avenue was purchased for establishment of a Catholic parochial school. The photograph shows Sacred Heart School at 406 West Iron Avenue in 1908. The St. Mary parish was built in 1956 at 230 East Cloud Street. By the end of the 2006 school year, all Catholic parochial school classes were held at the St. Mary and Sacred Heart buildings at 234 and 304 East Cloud Street. The building on Iron Avenue continues to be used for other religious education.

The first Catholic school in Salina opened at the Sacred Heart parish hall in 1879. In the fall of 1880, the Sisters of Charity took over the entire rectory while the resident pastor went to live with the Baier family on East Iron Avenue. In 1884, the Sacred Heart congregation acquired a house on the corner of Eighth Street and Iron Avenue, where this class photograph was probably taken, and added to it for a convent and classrooms.

This class is from Logan School in 1890. By 1887, Oakdale, South Park, and Logan Schools were built to accommodate the growing number of students crowding Central School. Logan School, on the southwest corner of Crawford and Front Streets, was torn down in 1910 because the city did not grow in that direction.

Shown here are students in Salina High School from the classes of 1886 through 1889. Although not in order, names of some of the scholars include Orestes Hopkins, Clarence Wight, Henry Lee Prescott, Fred Clark Prescott, James Hine, Anna R. Jennerson, Charles Burch, Ed Powers, Delia Bean, Maude Spencer, and Edith Sampson.

"Study first, outside issues afterwards" was the motto of every normal school student. Salina Normal University was established in 1883 on College Street at the west end of Iron Avenue. About 1,000 students attended during the school's 20 years of operation, completing studies in collegiate, normal, professional, musical, and fine arts. The building burned to the ground in 1904 and was not rebuilt.

This 1885 souvenir commencement program from Salina Normal University lists chorus presentations of "Oh the Merry Harvest Time" and "Though We Part."

FIRST ANNUAL

COMMENCEMENT ✦ EXERCISES

OF THE

Salina ✦ Normal ✦ University,

AT COLLEGE CHAPEL,

THURSDAY EVENING, JULY 2, 1885,

AT 8 O'CLOCK.

A group of uniformed cadets lines up in front of Vail Hall, St. John's first building, in 1889. St. John's Military School, on the northern edge of Salina, was founded by Bishop Thomas in 1887 as an Episcopal boarding academy for boys aged 8 to 18, where "Old Boys" tradition, military school bearing, and expectation were established.

Fortresslike Vail Hall, built in 1888 and enlarged in 1904, was a longtime fixture on the grounds of St. John's Military School. Vail was destroyed by fire on November 16, 1978. A $4 million Vanier Hall was dedicated on May 9, 2008. The Vanier barracks on the north side of the campus houses 132 cadets and replaced Mize Hall across campus. Vanier Hall has the latest in recreational equipment, including home theaters, PlayStations, and three pool tables lined with felt in orange and black, the school colors.

In 1885, Col. William Phillips chose the highest hill on the east side of Salina to build a palatial home for his second wife, Anna. After William Phillips's death in 1893, the home was converted to the Mount Barbara Military Academy. The academy was organized for the purpose of giving instruction in academic and commercial subjects along with military training, operating from the site from 1899 to 1901, when lightning struck the building causing it to burn to the ground.

In 1898, when the world depended on newspapers for information, Pres. William McKinley called for volunteers to respond to the troubles between Cuba and Spain. The 85 Salina volunteers received a very patriotic and touching farewell. When the Spanish-American War was over, celebrations were given to honor the returning soldiers. Charles Pratt (pictured), Samuel L. Wilson, and Henry Morrison were killed in action. Wilson H. McAllister died of disease; typhoid fever prevailed in all the U.S. camps.

In 1895, photographer F. A. Loomis appropriately used a bicycle to frame brothers Frank and Fred Eberhardt, who won awards and prizes in bicycling. Frank held three world records in bicycling.

Bicycling became popular for recreation as well as competition in the 1880s. The Salina Bicycle Club was the largest in the state prior to 1900. Seventy young men joined the Salina Bicycle Club in 1895, when the dues were dropped from $5 to $2.50. The oval bicycle racing track, inside the horse racing track at Oakdale Park, was the fastest in the state.

Atherton studio captured Estella Low in 1909. Low was active in the operation of Low Drug Store, founded in 1909 by her brother Henry Low, who passed away in 1925. Low Drug was a popular gathering place because of the ice-cream and soft drink fountain it maintained into the late 1950s. Estella and her sister Emma Low were partners with Norb Skelly at the pharmacy, 106 South Santa Fe Avenue, which closed in the late 1990s.

ATHERTON    SALINA, KANS.

With water standing in the background, a group of young people pose for a picture around the Oakdale Park fountain, summer of 1891. While many changes have occurred in Oakdale Park, the restored fountain remains.

Around 1900, a band parades south on Santa Fe Avenue near the Ash Street intersection. The unique structure in the background was built in the mid-1880s as the fraternal organization Knights of Pythias hall at 200 North Santa Fe Avenue. By 1903 the Salina Candy Company occupied the building with other businesses, including the Salina Daily Union newspaper.

Volunteer firefighters parade down Santa Fe Avenue for the 1899 Street Fair. Gaily decorated booths line both sides of the street with free shows, music, and exhibits. Firefighters held annual events for marching, games of competition, timed contests, and races, and ended the day with a dance. Salina hosted the Kansas State Volunteer Firefighters Association tournament in 1888.

# *Three*

# A NEW CENTURY
## 1900–1929

Santa Fe Avenue, Salina, Kansas.

Downtown Salina was a busy place at the dawn of the 20th century. This *c.* 1908 photograph, taken at the northeast corner of Santa Fe and Iron Avenues, gives the viewer a flavor of life at the time. Stevenson's Clothing Store, pictured in the center, was founded by Robert Burns Stevenson on March 1, 1896. His brother W. B. "Mac" Stevenson was known for his creative window displays, including one with men's red underwear and hand-tied cravats.

"Out of 36 autos in town here is a picture of 22 of them," stated the postcard mailed in 1907. Notice the child seated at the very front of the automobile. The postcard ended with a note that the sender's automobile was not in the photograph, as it was being repaired. Fred Shellabarger brought the first automobile to Salina in 1898, a secondhand Duryea that cost $750.

Taking his family for a drive is George Watson and his chauffeur. It was a common practice at the time for wealthier families to have chauffeurs. An article in the June 2, 1908, *Salina Semi-weekly Journal*, "Farmer Boys Want to Learn Honk Wagon Business," stated that many young men from the farm dreamed of an easy life as a chauffeur.

Laying tracks for gas streetcar travel is underway in this photograph in 1904. Allnut and Son operated the gasoline car service. It later became the Salina Street Railway Company and ran until 1910. The first streetcar travel was drawn by mules or horses in 1886–1887, operated by A. J. Anderson. By 1891, electric streetcars were introduced.

Trolley Car, Salina's Street & Interurban Ry.

All aboard! By 1916, streetcar travel was well established in Salina. The Salina Street and Interurban Railway had nine motor trolleys in addition to several trailers. Kansas Wesleyan University students could board the trolley on Santa Fe Avenue and ride it to Ash Street and then take the Union Station loop to the newly built depot. Many businesses opened quickly around Union Station, making this vicinity Salina's first outlying shopping center.

Salina's first fire chief, Fred Brodbeck, and driver Ray Miller are pictured here in the Mitchell fire automobile purchased in 1912. The automobile was converted into a one-of-a-kind firefighting machine. During his tenure, Brodbeck formed the Wesleyan Volunteer Fire Department to lend assistance in case of a fire in that part of the city; introduced inspections of all public buildings; and purchased new equipment, including a smoke and ammonia helmet.

"Go easy boys, my leg is broken," said Fire Chief Fred Brodbeck after sustaining a severe injury on September 30, 1912. He and Ray Miller were on their way to a fire when Miller swerved in an attempt to miss a wagon. Brodbeck died five days later from blood poisoning at the age of 39 and is buried at Gypsum Hill Cemetery. His headstone is engraved with a fire helmet.

The suffragettes' parade was held to garner support for equal suffrage. In 1887, Kansas women could vote in municipal and school elections. In November 1912, a vote was taken in Kansas to support the Equal Suffrage Amendment. Saline County voted no, the state voted yes. The 19th Amendment gave women the right to vote and was ratified nationwide on August 18, 1920.

The elaborately decorated Overland automobile, driven by Margaret Ollinger, appeared at the weeklong Salina Fall Festival held September 22–27, 1913. The car was covered with white batting and trimmed with red poppies, while a child rode in the rear seat and held ribbon streamers fastened to the hood of the car. The car won a $15 prize. WCTU stands for the Woman's Christian Temperance Union.

Hand in hand, Pat Crawford and Alice Schwartz safely cross Santa Fe Avenue with traffic officer Andy Logan in 1927. Years later, Crawford recalled, "We walked nine blocks back and forth to school every day . . . and at lunch, too! We weren't allowed to cross until Andy Logan came to help us."

The second courthouse was built in 1912–1913 on the same site as the first courthouse, located at North Ninth Street between Park and Elm Streets. It served until the present city-county building was occupied in November 1969 at 300 West Ash Street. Today this building is home to the Saline County Commission on Aging and the Salina Senior Center.

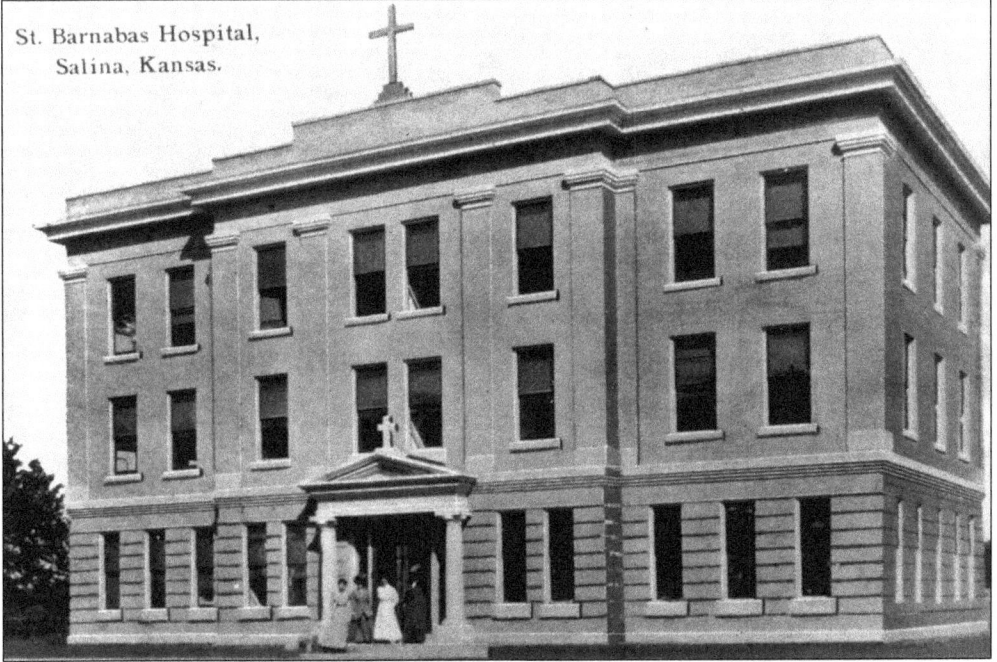

St. Barnabas Hospital,
Salina, Kansas.

St. Barnabas Hospital, located on the grounds of St. John's Military School, was built in 1909 as larger hospital facilities were needed in Salina. Built under the leadership of Bishop Sheldon Griswold of the Episcopal Church, the hospital cost approximately $30,000 and opened in 1910. Due to financial and staffing problems, St. Barnabas was closed in 1922 and later used by the St. John's Military School until 1965, when it was razed.

St. John's Hospital, the first $100,000 building in Salina, was opened in 1914. Located at 141 North Penn Avenue, the Catholic hospital was planned by the Sisters of St. Joseph of Concordia, Kansas. The building was made of red paving brick, steel construction, and white glazed terra-cotta trimmings, and could accommodate 87 patients. The first year the hospital treated 400 patients. (Courtesy of Audrey Peterson.)

The 1926 class of Asbury School of Nursing pictured here includes, from left to right, (first row) Miss Bauchop, Mrs. Stauffer, and Miss Starns; (second row) Miss Birdwell, Miss Sigler, superintendent Florence A. Braddick, supervisor Mrs. Jackson, and Miss Woodward. Pathology, public sanitation, ethics, psychology, and first aid were some of the subjects taught at the school.

# ASBURY
# PROTESTANT HOSPITAL
## Salina, Kansas.

"Asbury hospital was crowded from the beginning," stated the pamphlet. To meet the medical needs of Salina and surrounding communities, the hospital sought financial support to build an additional six floors. The first unit was completed in April 1927. In 1995, Asbury and St. John's Hospitals merged and formed the Salina Regional Health Center.

46

In 1903, the Carnegie Free Library opened at the southwest corner of Eighth and Iron Streets. Andrew Carnegie generously donated $15,000 for the building, and the City of Salina provided 3,000 books and maintenance on the building. An addition was built in 1922 to the south end of the library and served the city until 1968, when the current library at 301 West Elm Street was opened. The building was razed in 1969.

Early librarians at the Salina Public Library at 102 South Eighth Street, from left to right, are Alice Miller, Louise Davidson, Delia Brown (head), Renna MacGilrary (assisting librarian), Mary Zill, and Kirsten Atherton. Mr. VanDoren was the library's custodian. In 1915, the library boasted of owning 13,000 volumes. Brown served as librarian from 1904 until November 1945 and was very active in women's organizations.

The "Birthplace of the Meridian Highway US 81" marker, located at the corner of North Fifth and Otis Streets, was due in part to Salina businessman Winfield W. Watson. He helped organize the highway by often spending his own funds for highway markers. The Meridian Highway ran from Winnipeg, Canada, to Mexico City, better known as U.S. 81 and Interstate 35. The marker is no longer intact.

Pictured here are the owners and employees of Salina Automobile Company. Arthur J. Cleveland and Harry A. Brownlee, owners and general agents for Buick and Hudson automobiles, had their garage located at 212–214 North Santa Fe Avenue. "Repair work, a specialty" was the motto stated in their Salina City Directory advertisement of 1915.

Salina's first chautauqua assembly was held at Oakdale Park on July 14, 1906, with many speeches and musical fare. The assembly lasted many days and cleared $560.34 profit. During World War I, the annual event was cancelled but resumed in July 1920. It was a grand time to visit with friends, be entertained, and relax under the shady trees and tents. In many ways it was a precursor to today's Smoky Hill River Festival.

Claflin Hall was built in 1901 at Oakdale Park in part to host the annual chautauqua assembly. The facility could accommodate up to 3,500 people. The first chautauqua was held in 1874 at Lake Chautauqua, New York, and was a national phenomenon. The annual chautauqua provided time for folks to enjoy athletic events, Bible study groups, educational opportunities, musical entertainments, and gifted speakers.

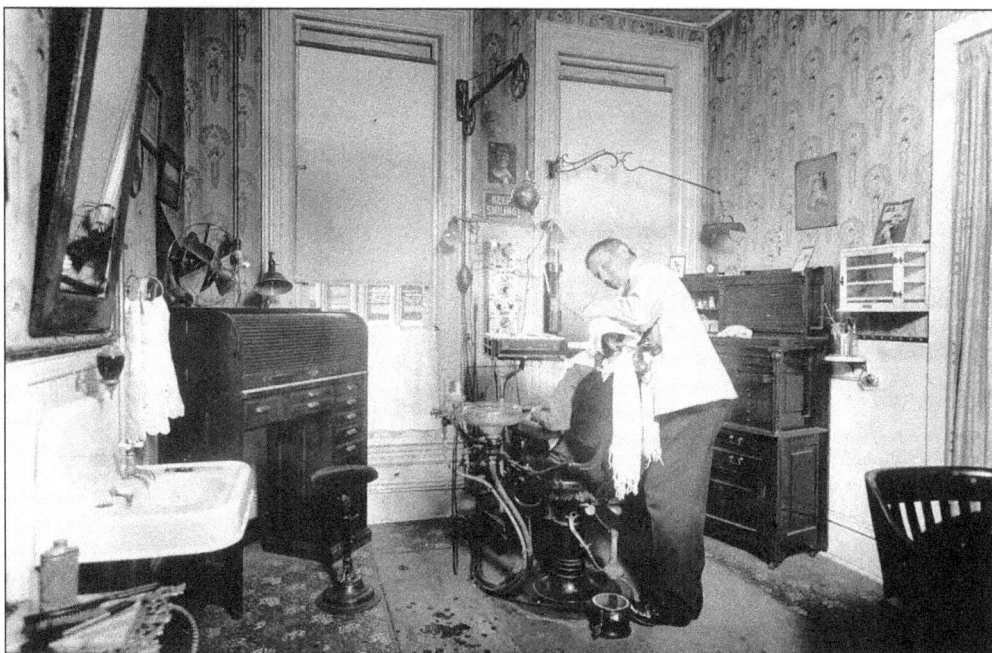

Dr. James H. Walker and a patient are pictured here in his dental office located at 108 North Santa Fe Avenue around 1910. By that time the X-ray machine for dental use had been introduced, as well as the use of Novocain. Dr. Walker practiced dentistry from 1899 until his death in 1942.

Need a haircut, shoes shined, or a bath? Located on the west side of Santa Fe Avenue, across from today's Bank of America building, Knight's Barber Shop, owned by Tom and Stella Knight, was the place to go. The shelf in the back of the room held customers' shaving mugs. In the 1920s, the Knights purchased a five-chair shop at 132 North Santa Fe Avenue, which included a beauty shop for women in the back.

S. J. Strickler began his jewelry store operation in 1884. In 1910, he sold it to his son, Benjamin A., who sold the business to Vernon Webster in 1944. The store, located at 123 North Santa Fe Avenue and known as Vernon Jewelers, is in the same location today. Both men were involved in church, business, and social organizations.

Gates Grocery Store opened on July 15, 1899, and was one of many home-owned grocery stores. In 1901, the store moved to 102 Santa Fe Avenue. John Gates, owner, won a $50 first-place prize in September 1915, for the window display highlighting Welch Grape Juice Week. Gates then turned over the prize to Will Cubberly, the window decorator.

Beginning in 1872, Seitz Eagle Drug Store had a long and rich history dispensing medicines, general drugs, and other sundries. Oscar Seitz, considered one of the wealthiest men in Salina, was the first owner, followed by his eldest son, Charles, at the dawn of the 20th century. The drugstore was located at 102 North Santa Fe Avenue until its closing in September 1946, when it was sold to C. V. Crosswy.

In 1882, telephone service arrived in Salina, with 24 subscribers. On January 1, 1895, the Salina Telephone Company, located at 109 South Santa Fe Avenue, was formed, and membership grew from 75 to 225 in one year, at a cost of $1 per month. Phoebe Bowen was the first independent telephone operator. At the close of the 1920s, the number of subscribers had risen to 5,772.

Shellabarger Mill & Elevator Co., Salina, Kansas.

In 1881, David Shellabarger bought the Salina Mill and Elevator Company. The mill at that time produced 150 barrels of ground wheat daily. Later his son Fred became manager and in 1906 changed the name to Shellabarger Mill. At its peak, the company owned and operated mills in Salina and Clay Center and had 38 elevators, producing up to 3,000 barrels of flour each day and storing over 1.5 million bushels of wheat. The company was sold in 1949.

Hauling grain to town in his automobile, the man on this postcard represents the change in agriculture from horse-drawn cart to horseless carriage. The mill took the grain and ground it into flour and other products necessary for everyday life. Behind the automobile is the First Church of Christ Scientist meeting place at Eighth and Mulberry Streets, established in 1909.

"The Jayhawk"
TRADE MARK REG.

CATALOG
49

SINCE 1903
★

HAY TOOLS
HYDRAULIC LOADERS

LOW COST YEAR 'ROUND
PORTABLE POWER for the FARM

SINCE
1903
▼

THE WYATT MANUFACTURING CO.
SALINA, KANSAS

In 1902, Frank Wyatt, farmer and inventor, produced the Jayhawk Stacker, revolutionizing hay-making methods. He moved to Salina in 1903 and began the Wyatt Manufacturing Company. The stacker was known for cutting down the farmer's labor and expense, making the implement a favorite of farmers for many years. In 1972, the company's stock was sold to a group of Salina businessmen headed by Q. A. Applequist.

54

Something sweet for Salina, in 1903 the Salina Candy Company began the business of making confections. Located on the corner of Santa Fe Avenue and Ash Street, its building looked like a castle, complete with a turret. The factory manufactured confections, including bon-bons doused with chocolate, caramel, or butterscotch, then dusted with a thin powder to prevent sticking.

H. D. Lee Mercantile Company was the first wholesale company in Salina. Henry D. Lee started his road to success with $1.50 and worked as a teacher, hotel clerk, realtor, and businessman. Due to ill health, he sought a place to recuperate and selected Salina for its health-giving climate. Both buildings netted 15,000 square feet of floor space. Lee died in 1928.

Glen Martin, Aviator, Salina, Kans.

The first airplane flight in Salina took place on a gray autumn day in 1911 near Kansas Wesleyan University by one-time resident Glenn L. Martin in his 850-pound biplane. The airplane had a wingspan of 34 feet and was powered by a 30-horsepower Eldridge engine located at the back of the pilot's neck. Flaps between the wings tilted the plane. Those watching were thrilled to see history in the making.

PHOTO by MAGERKURTH

Glenn L. Martin, pioneer aviator and entrepreneur and schooled in Salina, was the founder of Martin-Marietta and Lockheed Martin aerospace companies. He was noted for many "firsts," including flying an airplane under its own power on August 1, 1908; developing a successful parachute; and completing an air mail flight; later his company built and launched a man-made satellite. The Kansas Wesleyan University athletic field was named Martin Stadium for his generous support.

Due to difficult financial conditions, Kansas Wesleyan University's Pioneer Hall took several years to complete. The administration building was dedicated the "Hall of Pioneers" on September 15, 1930.

With two students, two instructors, one typewriter, and less than $100 invested in crude tables and chairs, Kansas Wesleyan Business College began. By 1907, 1,000 students were enrolled at the Roach Building on the corner of Santa Fe Avenue and Walnut Street. In 1935, the business college transferred its program and activities to Kansas Wesleyan University.

This 1929 aerial photograph of the million-dollar Marymount College building shows its sheer size and beauty. Dedicated in June 1922, the Sisters of St. Joseph of Concordia conducted the school until 1942. Boasting 300 rooms and a capacity for 500 female students, the college hosted a grade school, high school, and college. In 1968, the college became coeducational. Due to financial troubles, the college closed its doors in May 1989.

The two-story Washington High School, located at the corner of Third and Mulberry Streets, cost $76,000. From 1910 to 1952, "Old Washington" educated many Salina students. In the fall of 1953, students attended the newly built Salina High School, now called Salina Central High School. The Washington building was then used for elementary students, school administration offices, the county health department, and the recreation commission until 1972, when the building was razed.

By 1914, the school board saw the need for an additional school. Lincoln Junior High School, located between Seventh and Eighth Streets, was built for $73,901 and dedicated in honor of Abraham Lincoln's birthday, February 12, 1917. Today Lincoln Junior High School is now the Pioneer President's Place apartments.

Reading, writing, and arithmetic were some of the subjects taught in this fifth-grade classroom at Oakdale School in the early 1900s. The desks were hard, and lessons were taught from well-worn books. The teachers were usually young, single women who lived under strict guidelines, including no smoking; wearing at least two petticoats; not wearing brightly colored dresses; not leaving town without permission; and keeping the schoolroom neat and clean.

The children in this photograph were students in the kindergarten class at Oakdale School. The program was progressive and helpful to children. The classroom furnishings included Milton Bradley tables, Mosher chairs in varying heights, educational materials, and many good toys such as dolls, furniture, and dishes, said to be one of the most natural motives to work and play.

The 1907 Second Ward School class photograph shows the diversity of races represented in Salina at the time. The school, located on West Elm Street between Seventh and Eighth Streets, was later renamed Longfellow School. The building was torn down in 1945.

Christ's Cathedral, Salina, Kansas.

Bishop Sheldon M. Griswold began the long building process of Christ Cathedral with the turning of the first sod on Monday, April 2, 1906. Griswold noted in his address to the District of Salina that the new cathedral "stands before all else for the glory of God, and, secondly, it is for your use." The building, designed in an early Gothic style, with the walls made entirely of stone, was consecrated on Ascension Day, May 28, 1908, and is in use today.

St. John's Lutheran Church, Salina, Kansas.

On March 6, 1916, St. John's English (Evangelical) Lutheran Church began the process of building a larger church building with the sale of its property at Santa Fe Avenue and Walnut Street. One year later, on May 13, 1917, the congregation marched in joyous celebration to the new building at 302 South Seventh Street, where they continue to worship today. The total cost for the building and furnishings was $46,169.46. (Courtesy of Audrey Peterson.)

Monday, June 1, 1903, began the torrent of rain, flood, and disaster for Salina and surrounding communities. In one day alone, five and a quarter inches of rain fell, causing buildings to collapse, supply trains to stop, 26 extra policemen to be deputized to prevent pilfering, and great loss of stock and personal property. Emergency committees were established to supply food and shelter for the homeless. Fortunately, few deaths were reported.

On August 17, 1927, the *Salina Journal* reported that in a short time the floodwaters at the Walnut Street Bridge had risen 21.5 inches. Automobiles were moved close to homes ready to be called into action. Delivery boys carried groceries in baskets on top of their heads, and ducks were reported swimming in front yards. Seventy National Guardsmen were called out to help. The flood left 100 Salina residents homeless.

62

The Current Literature Club was organized in 1894 as a study and culture club and strove to help with civic and community improvements. The club represents active women's organizations of this period. Included in this c. 1920 photograph are Mrs. Frank Hageman, Catherine Eberhardt, Delia Brown, May Belleville Brown, Mrs. R. P. Cravens, Alice G. Bond, Emily Putnam, and Mrs. Charles Kirtland.

This early-1900s baseball team included J. J. Eberhardt, ? Carkhoff, ? Behan, C. C. Eberhardt, ? Loeb, ? Brown, H. A. Ley, ? Reed, ? Gammons, ? Allis, and ? Hyde. Notice the style of the players' clothing, athletic shoes, catcher's mitt, baseball, and trophy. The building in the background is probably Claflin Hall, once located at Oakdale Park.

LAMER HOTEL, SALINA, KANSAS

Built on the northwest corner of Santa Fe Avenue and Ash Street, the Lamer Hotel (1915–1965) began its life as the National Hotel in 1887. The Lamer had the reputation of being the "hub of the social and business life of our town." Within the brick walls of the four-story hotel, government leaders, musicians, actors, and the social elite gathered, as did newspaper reporters. Fancy parties, receptions, and great food were always on hand.

WARREN HOTEL, SALINA, KANSAS                                                    1395-29

Hotel Warren, a seven-story, 70-room building located on the corner of Eighth and Ash Streets, opened for business on August 9, 1928. Known for its "home-note" touches, many people felt a sense of welcome through the elegant furnishings, interior decoration, and arrangement. The hotel was sold in 1963 and became the Gold Key Apartment Building, still in use today.

64

Memorial Hall, Salina, Kans.

A 1929 postcard of Memorial Hall shows the size and beauty of the building designed by Charles W. Shaver as a monument to "our veterans of all wars." On the first floor were the ladies' retiring room, men's lounging room, a portable stage, and a room with a seating capacity of 3,073. The second floor housed many club meeting rooms. Since 1993, Memorial Hall has been the home of Community Access Television.

Will Rogers was one of many entertainers who graced the Memorial Hall stage. Others included the Paul White Orchestra that played for Salina High School commencement ceremonies in 1925; Tipca Orchestra of Mexico in 1927; the United States Army Band; and the Russian Symphony Choir in 1929.

# WILL ROGERS

Auspices
## American Legion
Memorial Hall                    April 30, 1928

65

Convention Hall    Salina Kans.

"Largest and best equipped stage in Kansas," boasted this postcard from the United Commercial Travelers Convention Hall, located at the northwest corner of Santa Fe Avenue and Walnut Street. The building cost $49,480.89 and was in use from 1907 to 1946. Ticket costs in 1907 ranged from 25¢ to $1. Franklin D. Roosevelt, William Jennings Bryant, Edgar Bergen, and Charlie McCarthy are just a few of the celebrities who graced the convention hall stage.

The United Commercial Travelers organization brought convention groups and other businesses to its convention hall, helping to put Salina on the map. A fraternal organization, it provided moral support and material aid to its members, established a widow and orphan reserve fund, worked for better conditions for traveling salesmen, and assisted in establishing the white center line painted on highways.

The Grand Theatre, shown in a postcard dated 1929, was the former United Commercial Travelers Convention Hall. Located on the northwest corner of Santa Fe Avenue and Walnut Street, it was known as the "swanky" theater. Scrawled on the walls of the old dressing rooms were the names of many famous celebrities. High school graduations and other festivals took place at the "Grand." Katherine Ladd bought the property in 1946.

Howell's Boys Band later became the current Salina Municipal Band. This *c.* 1913 photograph shows boys wearing uniforms secured from funds donated by local businessmen. The band's leader, T. S. Howell, initially called the band "Howell Jayhawker Boys Band." The city built a band shell for the group in 1916 near Washington High for $3,200. The band performed there until 1938, when it was destroyed by fire.

The Memorial Day parade held on May 30, 1908, was led by the Salina Military Band and Company M of the 5th Kansas Militia, followed by members of the Grand Army of the Republic marching to musical numbers in "slow time." Upon reaching the Iron Street Bridge, the Civil War veterans received a ride to Gypsum Hill Cemetery where children placed floral decorations at the monument of the unknown dead and the graves of all 148 Union soldiers buried there.

In 1918, 1st Lt. George S. Robb won the Congressional Medal of Honor award for outstanding service in World War I. During a battle near Sechault, France, he remained with his platoon, the 369th Infantry, 93rd Division, better known as the "Harlem Hellfighters." Following the war, Robb served as postmaster in Salina, and in 1935, he was elected state auditor. (Courtesy of the Kansas State Historical Society.)

"The De Luxe Canned Music of Yesterday" was a magic treat, reported Mrs. E. A. Hiller in the *Kansas City Star* newspaper on December 25, 1938. Each girl would put a nickel in the slot, adjust the ear pieces, and listen to music in a way they had not experienced before. Listening to the music are, from left to right, Lois Mitchell, Kitty Quincy, Ella Mitchell, Edna Eberhardt, Bertha Hoover, Mr. Mitchell, Vera Eberhardt, Nina Quincy, and Pearl Moore.

The Salina Raven Patrol was the first Boy Scout patrol to be enrolled in the United States. In the fall of 1909, F. John Romanes joined the staff of St. John's Military Academy and immediately began efforts to form a boys group patterned after the Boy Scouts movement in England. In January 1910, he established the Raven patrol. This photograph was taken in 1911 and shows the Raven and Eagle patrols in formation.

The pool staff pictured here would be very busy at the new $15,000 municipal pool, located at Oakdale Park. Opening on June 15, 1925, the 145-by-250-foot pool could accommodate 2,000 bathers. The pool was equipped with diving platforms, slippery slides, a sandy beach, dressing rooms, a first aid room, shower baths, and other amenities. A total of one million gallons of water was used each week to fill the pool.

The show must go on, even when an elephant goes mad. Snyder, the Sells-Floto Circus elephant, went "crazy" and chased the keepers, attendants, and the audience on September 13, 1920. A firing squad was formed, an audience was on hand, and down went the nine-ton animal. Plans were made to bury him, but no space was large enough. The carcass was skinned and used as fertilizer.

70

# *Four*

# TROUBLING TIMES
## 1930–1949

As the 1930s began, Santa Fe and Iron Avenues bustled with activity. Everyone was optimistic about the future. Salina ranked sixth in the United States in the production of hard winter wheat, and new buildings were going up. Salina's 20,127 inhabitants could not know that they stood at the threshold of the Great Depression, which would lead into World War II. Ironically, during the decade of the 1940s, Salina grew. Its population nearly doubled, and the town matured into a community with worldwide significance.

Arriving for a job at KSAL in the 1940s, Walter Neumann saw the 20-foot steel arch through the train window and decided its message was for him. In 1916, the Salina Chamber of Commerce had erected this boaster sign at the corner of Twelfth and Bishop Streets. It contained over 1,200 colorful bulbs, and the local electrical company agreed to its maintenance at no charge. The back side urged visitors to "Come again." The sign came down in 1954.

UNION PACIFIC STREAMLINER

The first streamliner passenger train in the United States made an appearance in April 1934 and was later dubbed the *City of Salina*. Spectators were surprised to see its canary yellow and golden brown hues. Although popular and relatively inexpensive to operate, the "bullet" train ran for only seven years between Salina and Kansas City. Just after the attack on Pearl Harbor in 1941, it was withdrawn from service and scrapped for its aluminum as part of the war effort.

72

The increase in automobile ownership naturally brought about an increase of dealerships in the community. By 1931, there were 15 dealers in passenger cars, predominantly located on North Seventh Street and North Santa Fe Avenue. Here Charles Adams, owner of Adams Oldsmobile Company at 128–220 North Seventh Street, prepares to give Fred Ridings, a local carpenter, a spin in this 1930 roadster.

In July 1939, Marshall Motor Company employed an impressive array of salesmen and mechanics at 743–749 North Santa Fe Avenue. Ward Marshall came to Salina from Clay Center, Kansas, in 1928 and established the Marshall Motor Company on North Seventh Street. When a fire destroyed that lot about 1932, he rebuilt at the North Santa Fe Avenue address. Marshall and his service department constructed an early auto transport vehicle, which he used to deliver automobiles to dealers in northwest Kansas.

In 1928, when Rae Rearwin, a Salina businessman, was building his first aircraft in a vacant garage, city officials and the chamber's aviation committee were buying 160 acres east of town from Mary Manning, W. F. Laessig, and Joseph Irving. This 1930s view of the first municipal airport captures the early days of city air. The airport closed on August 18, 1966. The old runway is still in use today as a stretch of Markley Road.

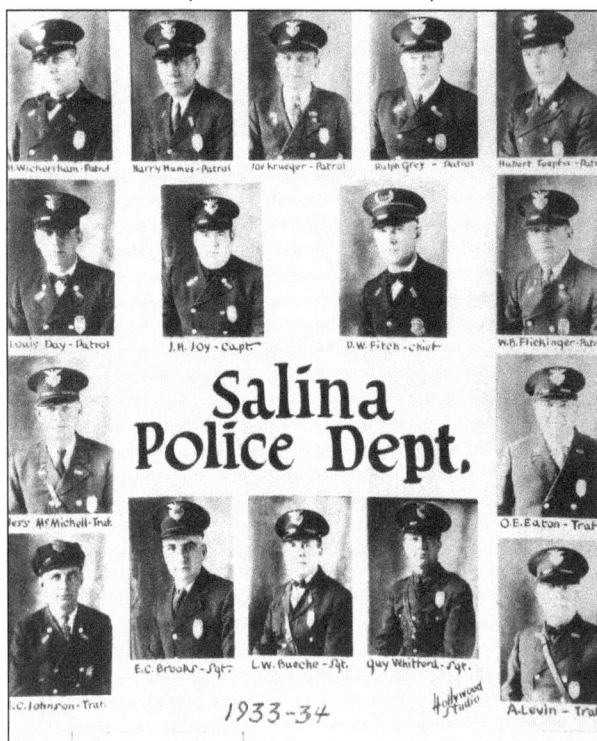

The Salina Police Department composite was taken in 1933–1934. From left to right, the officers are (top row) H. Wickersham, patrol; Harry Humes, patrol; Joe Krueger, patrol; Ralph Grey, patrol; and Robert Toepfer, patrol; (second row) Louis Day, patrol; Capt. J. H. Joy; Chief D. W. Fitch; and W. B. Flickinger, patrol; (third row) Jess McMickell, traffic and O. E. Eaton, traffic; (fourth row) E. C. Johnson, traffic; Sgt. E. C. Brooks; Sgt. L. W. Bueche; Sgt. Guy Whitford; and A. Levin, traffic.

When Salina City Hall was dedicated in July 1911, two of the five town founders were in attendance: James Muir and Alexander C. Spilman. The elaborate ceremonies included a band concert, a parade of past and present mayors and councilmen, and an address by Henry J. Allen. The city offices conducted business at the corner of Fifth and Ash Streets until the current government center was completed in 1969. The building was razed in 1971.

An estimated 4,000 people, coming from all parts of Kansas, attended the dedication of Salina's new post office on September 24, 1938. This view of the building, located at 211 West Iron Avenue, shows the two carved stone figures flanking the main entrance. These were completed by sculptor Carl C. Mose of St. Louis, Missouri, after the building opened. The official names of the limestone sculptures were Land (man) and Communication (woman and child).

In 1881, roller mills replaced the stones for grinding grain, and with other innovative equipment, wheat flour became a refined and sought-after product. By 1939, five mills produced a total capacity of 17,000 hundredweight of flour daily, and Salina ranked fourth in the nation as a flour-producing center. Shown in this 1924 photograph are four of the five milling companies.

The Lee and Warren Milling Company mill was built by commercial magnate Henry D. Lee and George F. Warren in 1899 at 350 North Seventh Street. The company marketed its flour throughout the United States and to England, France, Germany, Holland, and Puerto Rico. After 1918, it became known as the H. D. Lee Flour Mill, and in the 1940s, John J. Vanier purchased the business and changed the name to Weber Flour Mills Company, the former Weber mill having burned.

From left to right are Shellabarger Mill and Elevator Company, Robinson Milling Company, Weber Flour Mills Company, and H. D. Lee Flour Mills Company. The fifth, Western Star Mill Company, is the only one remaining today at the corner of Ash and Third Streets. It is now owned by ADM Milling Company.

Through the years, Salina's location as a crossroads has been ideal for investors in wholesale businesses. The Sutorius Bread Company began about 1925 when a group of men from Newton, Kansas—Oscar Sutorius, John Weber, and John Tourtellott—started a company that distributed Pan-Dandy bread to grocery stores in central Kansas. The business continued to operate until 1960 at 521 Bishop Street.

*finished 1929 — Dec & Jan 1930*   1397.29

On January 2, 1930, the United Life Building at Iron Avenue and Seventh Street opened its doors for a three-day "house warming." Visitors admired the Carthage marble corridors, arcade walls, and the terrazzo floors, cared for by a crew of 10 janitors. A mail chute connected every floor with outlets to a letterbox on the main floor. The city's tallest building was built by the United Life Insurance Company and designed by Charles Shaver.

In the early days, the town's water supply involved the Smoky Hill River and a well dug by Alexander Campbell at the intersection of Santa Fe and Iron Avenues. But since 1883, the municipal waterworks has been located at Fifth and South Streets. In 1935, Charles Shaver designed the remodeling of the water plant. Limestone ashlar adorns the doorway and front corners of the building. Art deco and crisscross brickwork decorate its cornice.

Upon graduating with the class of 1915 at Kansas State University, Charles Shaver, prominent Midwest architect, began his practice in Salina. Noted as a church architect, Shaver was honored many times by members of his profession. He was admitted to the Church Architectural Guild of America, a rare honor for a Midwesterner. His personal philosophy was to design beautiful, functional, and affordable buildings. Shaver died on March 6, 1961. (Courtesy of the Smoky Hill Museum.)

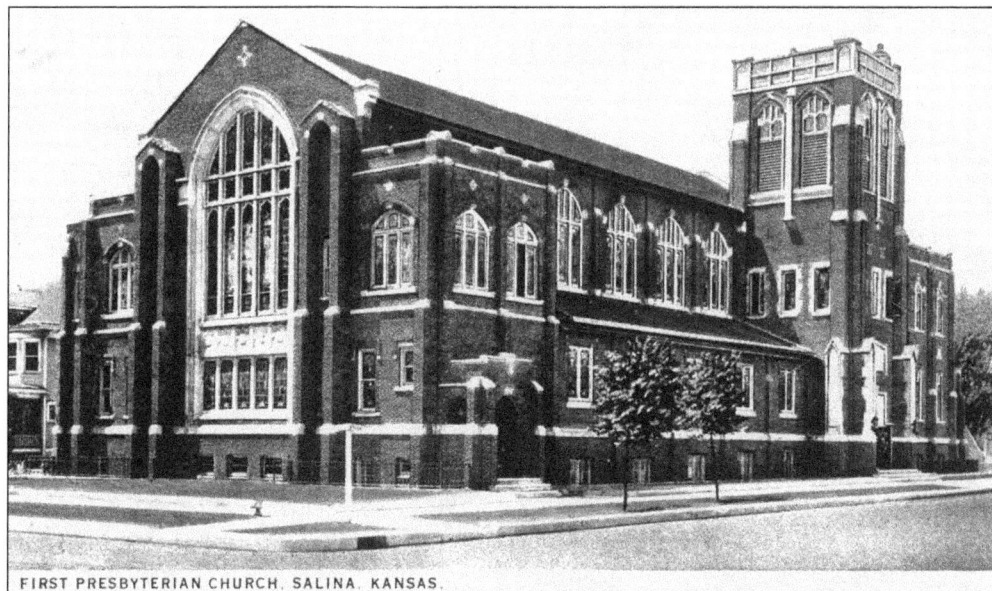

FIRST PRESBYTERIAN CHURCH, SALINA, KANSAS.

The First Presbyterian Church, 308 South Eighth, is one of Charles Shaver's many local church designs. In all, Shaver designed some 500 church buildings throughout the Midwest. This congregation is the oldest in Salina, its original members holding an organizational meeting on May 12, 1860. For 10 years, services took place in homes or meeting halls. Before this modified Gothic building was completed in 1923, two others had served: the first dedicated in 1871 and the second in 1893. (Courtesy of Audrey Peterson.)

Built around 1930, the Old Dutch Mill operated at the northwest corner of Santa Fe and Pacific Avenues. It remained a landmark for travelers on Highway 40 for over 30 years. The business was started by entrepreneur Nathan Jones and included a filling station, which sold Red Crown gasoline, a restaurant, and a tourist court or motel. This photograph may have been taken at its grand opening. It was demolished sometime in the 1960s.

In the spring of 1899, Mary West, age 30, and Lillian Hoyt, age 20, started out small at the rear of Farmer's National Bank on West Iron Avenue. The two were good business women, and their millinery shop continued to grow. Hoyt-West Millinery Company then moved to 123 North Santa Fe Avenue, where it employed 10 artistic milliners and trimmers. When Mary West died in 1931, Lillian Hoyt-Payne already owned the business and continued its operation. The store closed in the 1980s.

This building on the northeast corner of Santa Fe Avenue and Ash Street was originally the Knights of Pythias hall, built in the 1880s. In 1903, it became the Salina Candy Factory until about 1928. This photograph shows the Casa Bonita Café restaurant occupying the same building—minus the top two floors. In 1932, the medieval castle-style building was transformed to Spanish Mission–style and became home to the Casa Bonita Café and the union bus station. With the union bus station sharing a good portion of the building, this corner in downtown Salina was full of hustle and bustle. Uniformed waitresses and tables covered with white tablecloths gave the establishment a formal and inviting air that lasted into the early 1960s. The building was razed in 1981.

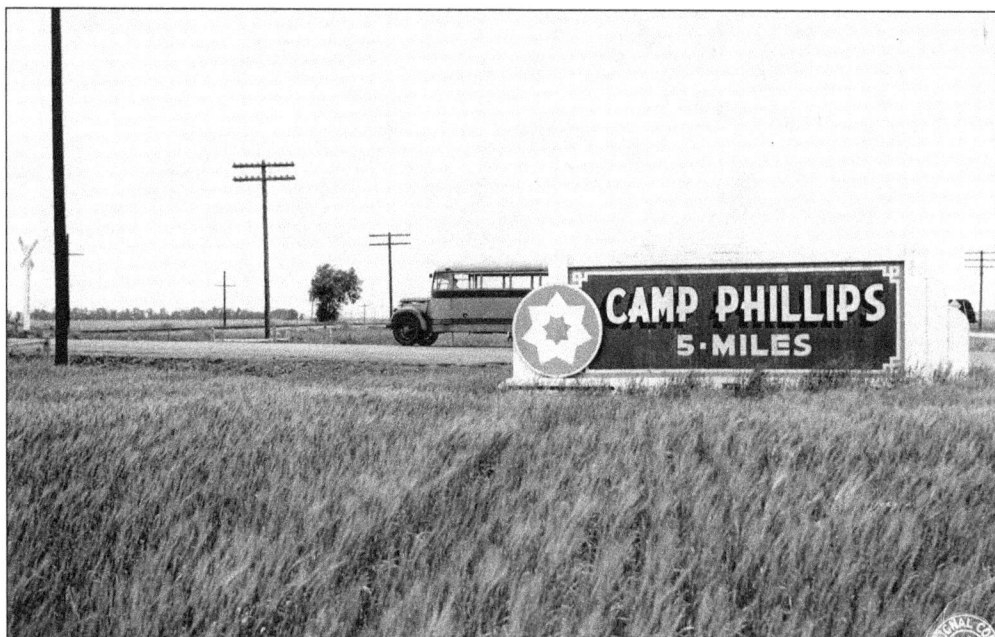

The United States entry into World War II set in motion circumstances that impacted Salina's future. Camp Phillips, located southwest of Salina, was a 46,000-acre army training installation. The base was activated in 1942 and officially deactivated 1944. One mile southwest of the cantonment was an internment camp for Italian and German war prisoners. Also called Camp Phillips, the compound had a capacity of 3,000 prisoners and operated from mid-1943 until late 1944.

Smoky Hill Army Air Field was used as a processing and staging area for heavy bombardment units going overseas. It became operational in December 1942. During the war years, it was equipped with B-17s and B-29s. The facility was located five miles south of Salina. In 1948, its name was officially changed to Smoky Hill Air Force Base, after the Army Air Corps became the United States Air Force.

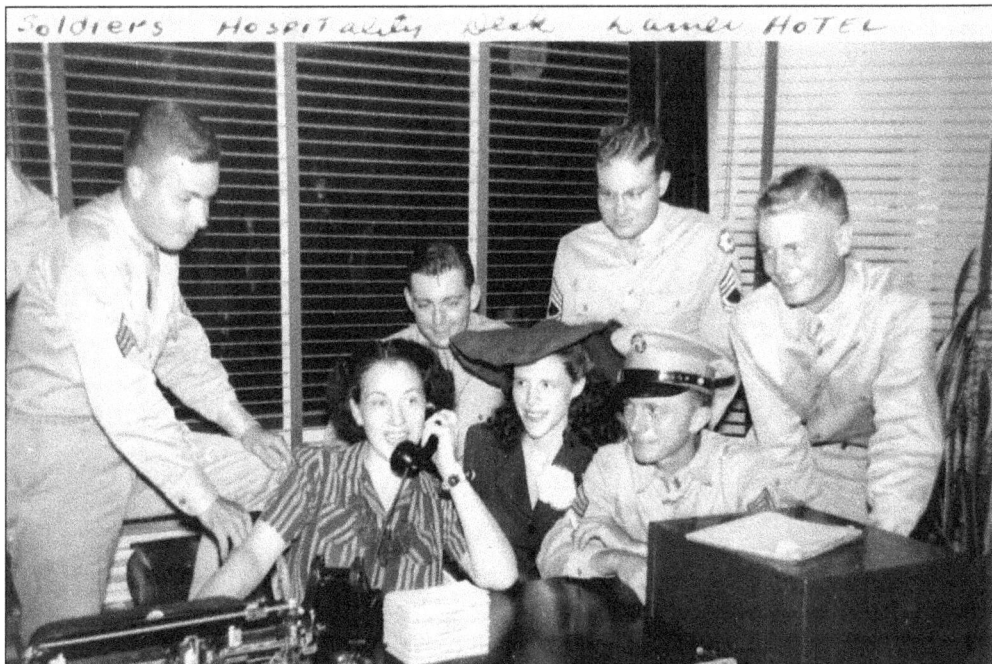

Soldiers Hospitality Desk Lamer Hotel

Once the war began in December 1941, life in Salina entered into an atypical period of time. This scene shows soldiers and young women gathering at a hospitality desk in the Lamer Hotel, located at the northwest corner of Santa Fe Avenue and Ash Street. The community interacted with the military in many ways through USO activities, church and school attendance, housing rentals, and civilian jobs at the military facilities.

Heavyweight boxing champion Joe Louis appears on Salina streets in a military visit by soldiers from Fort Riley, Kansas. Louis was in training at Fort Riley during 1942. While in the service, he used his influence to help African American soldiers gain acceptance in officers candidate school. (Photograph by Norb Skelly.)

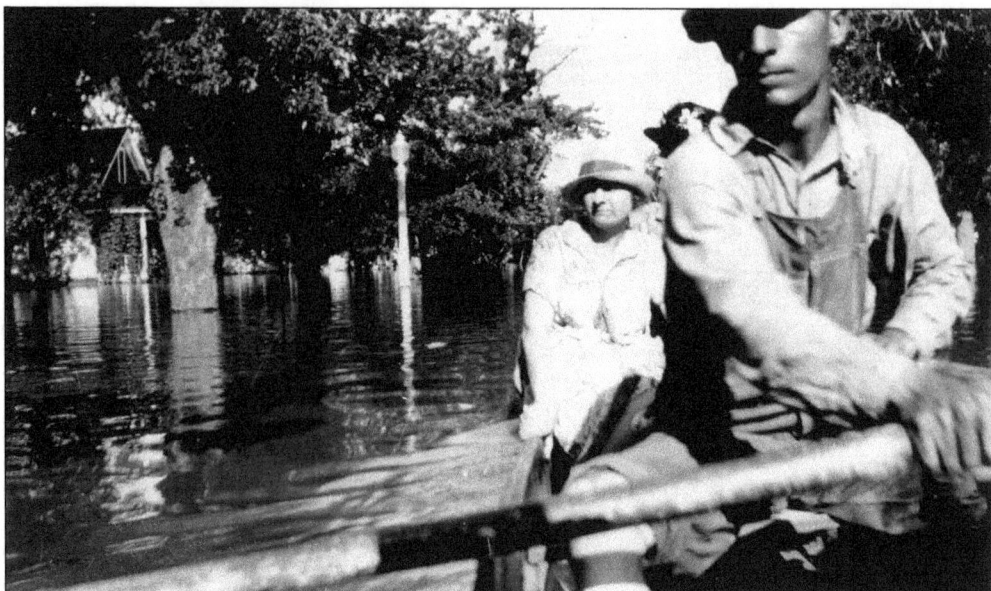

In addition to dust storms in the "Dirty Thirties," Salina also experienced floods in June 1938 and again in October 1941 that sent the Smoky Hill River over its banks. The Wiegner home at 636 East Iron Avenue served as a headquarters with patrol boats docking at the porch to deposit flood victims safely inside. Housewives in need of food or medical attention signaled passing boats from their porches, and word was relayed to the Wiegner house.

Two feet or more beneath these floodwaters lay Miller's field, the home of the Salina Millers, a member of the Western Association League and predecessor to the Salina Blue Jays. The photograph looks across right field and shows the agricultural hall at Kenwood Park in the background. During the 1938 flood, Red Cross stations opened in Memorial Hall at Ash and Ninth Streets for several days, taking in 70 to 250 refugees each night.

In 1917, a special bond election approved the purchase of 80 acres to build a new park. On October 1, 1930, Saline County's $30,000 agricultural hall was put to use for the first time when the Mid-Kansas Agricultural Live Stock and Horse Show opened in Kenwood Park. Charles Shaver was the architect for the building. The park was a busy place during the 1930s with horse races and baseball games, as well as agricultural meetings that brought out the automobiles.

One bright spot during the Depression years was the start of the trucking industry. When farming conditions grew dismal, William Davis earned a living with his long-distance hauling service. Other farm-to-market haulers did the same. William P. Graves trucked coal from southeast Kansas to Salina lumberyards and salt to Colorado bringing back produce. By the 1970s, his sons—William H., Dwight, John, and Lowell Graves—had developed the business into a multimillion-dollar company.

Despite the sacrifices that were made during these years, schoolchildren were indulged and happily took part in many festivities. May Day activities held in Oakdale Park attracted all schoolchildren. These Oakdale schoolgirls are dressed in their frilly dresses for the annual maypole dance that was part of the celebration, which included musical activities and the crowning of the May queen.

The second building for Oakdale School was built in 1930 at an approximate cost of $100,000. Charles Shaver designed the English Revival building, located on East Iron Avenue. The new building replaced the original one, which was built in 1887 in the middle of a cornfield. The small building on the far right of the photograph is the kindergarten cottage. The first private kindergarten class in Salina was inaugurated in 1909 by Jessie Miller Jodon.

Longfellow School, originally called Second Ward, was built in 1880 on the present site of the fire station on West Elm Street. It was needed to accommodate the increasing school population, which included the children of the many black families that were migrating from the south. It was not long before this building and "Old Central" became inadequate, necessitating the building of Oakdale School and Logan School, a short-lived school on Front Street.

In 1941, this fourth-grade class at Longfellow School contained an ethnic mix of students. In four more years the school building would be demolished. From left to right are (first row) Beverly Judson, Alvin Brockleman, Lucile Flammang, Delores Hunter, Pat Porter, and Jo Ann Bloomfield; (second row) Agnes Entz, Tommy Hernandez, Billy Walters, Joe Hernandez, Josephine Lopez, Connie Layman, and teacher Ann Marlin; (third row) Donald Roe, Raymond Sword, Marjorie Yent, Lupe Camerena, and Lupe Hernandez. The man in the photograph is unidentified.

While men joined fraternal organizations, professional groups, and civic clubs, women preferred cultural interest groups involving literature, music, art, and gardening. The ladies here may have belonged to the Art and Home Culture Club, the Musical Arts Group, or the Roundtable Club. Although hats were no longer favored for this kind of gathering, wearing one's Sunday best was appropriate for weekday outings.

Men spent their leisure time with outdoor activities, swimming, or playing handball at the local YMCA, pictured here. The building was dedicated on December 18, 1910, and stood on the southeast corner of Iron Avenue and Ninth Street. By the late 1940s, the facility had become inadequate to meet Salina's population growth. A building campaign began in 1952, and within four years, a gymnasium and swimming pool had been added.

The 1930s ushered in the age of motion picture theaters in Salina. The Jayhawk Theatre at 139 South Santa Fe Avenue was one of five downtown movie houses, which included the Fox Watson, Strand, Vogue, and Royal Theatres. In those days, in addition to the main feature, a person could watch cartoons, news reels, previews, short subjects, and an occasional travelogue, all running continuously while the theater was open.

The Fox Watson Theatre, on the National Register of Historic Places, opened in February 1931 at 155 South Santa Fe Avenue. Named for its founder W. W. Watson and the Fox Theater Company, the theater hosted film shows and live performances. When Dickinson Theaters closed the Fox Watson Theatre in 1987, it was sold to the City of Salina. After its restoration, it reopened as the Stiefel Theatre for the Performing Arts on March 8, 2003.

For nearly 30 years Club Cherokee was the place to be on a Friday night. The weekly dances began in the summer of 1943 against the backdrop of World War II. Sponsored by the YMCA and run by a council of high school kids from Salina High and Sacred Heart, the idea went over big with the teenagers of Salina. The name was catchy and was adopted from the theme song of

Charlie Barnet's Orchestra. At first the saddle shoe set danced in the basement of the Masonic temple, located at 340 South Santa Fe Avenue where USO dances also took place. Later, like the swinging group pictured here, they congregated on the roomy floor of Memorial Hall, which sat at the corner of North Ninth and West Ash Streets.

The Golden Waffle, later known as the Waffle Nook, sat at 227 South Santa Fe Avenue. In this 1948 photograph, the flowers suggest that the little café across the street from the Vogue Theatre might recently have had a grand opening. The man in the chef's hat is Jim Taylor, and he appears to be braced for a full house once the movie "lets out." Wonder which clock is right?

As the 1940s drew to a close, Salina joined the country in expressing a sense of optimism that the future would bring brighter times. The Salina Chamber of Commerce echoed this sentiment in its promotion of the town. Salina was poised to resume the role the town founders had envisioned. At the junction of two major roadways, the Meridian Highway (Highway 81) and the Golden Belt (Highway 40), the city was truly at America's crossroads.

# Five

# CHANGE IN THE AIR
## 1950–1979

Salina was enjoying prosperous times in the early 1950s. The New York Stock Exchange reached the highest level since 1929, and the fear of polio was lifted when Jonas Salk developed a vaccine against the disease. Salina was the major shopping hub between Topeka and Denver; locally owned downtown stores were filled with shoppers at Christmastime.

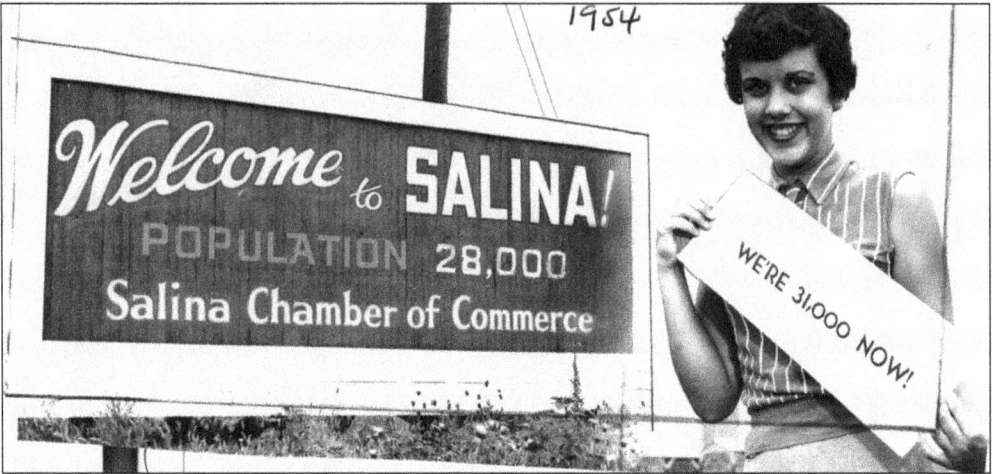

1954

Welcome to SALINA!
POPULATION 28,000
Salina Chamber of Commerce

WE'RE 31,000 NOW!

"Your opportunity: Where north and south meet east and west." Salina was one of the fastest-growing cities in Kansas in the early 1950s. Strategically located at the intersection of major federal Highways 40 and 81, and served by five railroads, Salina was the perfect home base for many regional and national businesses that took advantage of trucking and rail accessibility. The influx of military families at nearby Smoky Hill Air Force Base boosted the economy.

1958

EISNER BROS. INC.

FOX WATSON

FOX WATSON GARY COOPER IN "HIGH NOON"

When external sun visors covered two-piece windshields, Packards, Kaisers, and Studebakers joined Fords, Buicks, and Chevrolets on Santa Fe Avenue, seen here looking north from Walnut Street. Gary Cooper was named best actor for his 1953 role as Marshal Will Kane in *High Noon*, showing at the Fox Watson Theatre.

94

Built in 1957, Sacred Heart Cathedral replaced an older structure on the same Iron Avenue site between Eighth and Ninth Streets. The large circular pillars of light-colored native stone symbolize grain elevators that played an important part in development of Salina. The low relief sculpture with the wording "He who does not take up his cross and follow me is not worthy of me" was brought forward when the building was enlarged in 1999.

The area around Union Station at Bishop and Thirteenth Streets had been the hub of activity for many years. A lack of passengers and loss of profits due to competition from air and other modes of travel meant that the *Portland Rose* and many other passenger trains made their last runs through Salina before May 2, 1971. Congress passed the Rail Passenger Service Act at that time, which created Amtrak. The closest Amtrak station would be an hour away at Newton, Kansas.

In 1957, the former Smoky Hill Air Force Base southwest of Salina was renamed Schilling Air Force Base in honor of Col. David Schilling. A Kansan, Schilling became a World War II fighter pilot and made midair refueling for fighter aircraft a reality. Schilling died at age 38 in 1956 in an automobile accident in England.

"Peace Is Our Profession," spelled out here using soldiers in formation in 1960, was the Strategic Air Command motto. The Strategic Air Command, characterized by its bomber force from 1946 to 1992, retained its organization and mission after the Army Air Force became the U.S. Air Force in 1947. Schilling Air Force Base is most famous as the home of the 310th Strategic Bombardment Wing, which later became the 310th Strategic Aerospace Wing, flying B-47s until ceasing operations in 1965.

After the closure of Schilling Air Force Base in 1965, the unused property was set aside for wives and children of soldiers assigned to Vietnam. The women and children of Schilling Manor, sub-post home of the Waiting Wives of the United States armed forces, fought on the emotional home front during the Vietnam War. Since 1974 the manor has been used as public housing.

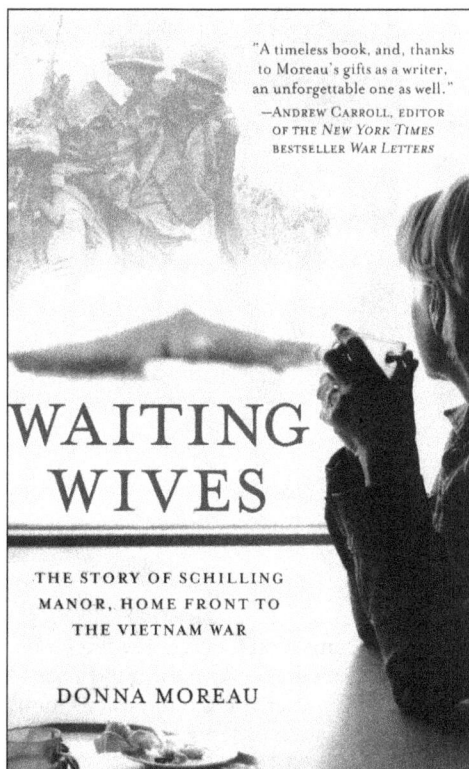

"A timeless book, and, thanks to Moreau's gifts as a writer, an unforgettable one as well."
—ANDREW CARROLL, EDITOR OF THE *NEW YORK TIMES* BESTSELLER *WAR LETTERS*

# WAITING WIVES

THE STORY OF SCHILLING MANOR, HOME FRONT TO THE VIETNAM WAR

DONNA MOREAU

Donna Lindsey Vanier, shown here with Col. David Schilling, dedicated the Boeing B-47 strato-jet *City of Salina* in 1954. Vanier also christened *City of Salina II*, a KC-135 refueling tanker in 1961, and *Thunderbolt of Salina*, an A-10, on January 23, 2008, making it the fourth aircraft to carry Salina's name. A B-17 had been named *The Salina* in 1944.

The Americanization Center, 433 North Front Street, was established in 1921 by the Women's Christian Temperance Union to aid Hispanic railroad workers and their families. The center closed in 1979 after the Community Chest, forerunner of the United Way, was developed to prevent duplication of services and develop cooperation of funded agencies.

"I like Ike, you like Ike, everybody likes Ike" was the jingle heard when Dwight D. Eisenhower campaigned for president in 1952. As the 34th president, Eisenhower began the interstate highway network, launched the space race, and added the words "under God" to the pledge of allegiance. The Dwight D. Eisenhower Presidential Library and Museum is in nearby Abilene, Kansas.

There were 36 commissioned officers on the police force in 1959 when police headquarters were located at 147 North Fifth Street. The department was moved to 255 North Tenth Street in 1969, where it has experienced some remodeling and expansion in recent years. Today's police department totals 109 employees, including management, administration, and the operating division.

Officer Herb Clark stands guard in front of the Montgomery Ward building, 131 North Santa Fe Avenue, during an investigation of a bomb scare. Clark is fondly remembered for his school visits as a ventriloquist. Montgomery Ward moved from downtown Salina to the Mid-State Mall, 2450 South Ninth Street, as an anchor store in 1972.

As beneficial as its location near a river had been for Salina's early settlers and growing businesses, the devastation caused by rising floodwaters occurred several times over the years, with major flooding in 1903 and 1951. Early in 1951, the city had received as much rain in 72 days as it normally accumulated in a year. A heavy rain on July 10, 1951, prompted evacuation of Salina residents; an estimated 1,800 people sought shelter.

Floodwaters engulfed sprawling Salina in 1951, when the new high school was under construction on Crawford Street between Front and Roach Streets. Today the city draws about 60 percent of its water supply directly from the river; the river's subflow serves to recharge the city's water wells. Salina was reminded of its reliance on the river in the drought of 2006 when the wells reached low levels, resulting in water rationing.

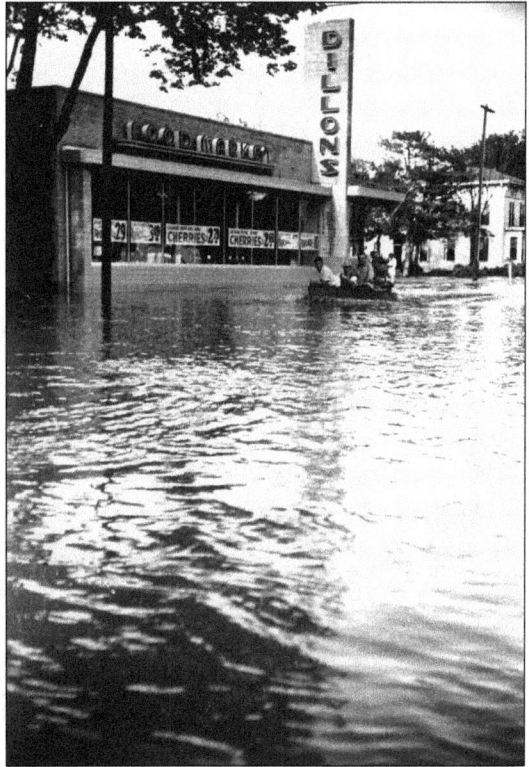

Dillon's grocery store, 511 East Iron Avenue, is shown surrounded by 1951 floodwater. The 1951 disaster caused Congress to take action. After many years in the planning, the flood protection designed to divert floodwaters from Salina was completed in 1962. The Smoky Hill River cutoff channel diverted the flow of water around the city. The Corps of Engineers built miles of levee, right-of-way easements, and bridge changes around the city. The City of Salina continues to maintain the 39 miles of flood control system. The Kanopolis Reservoir southwest of Salina has offered additional flood control, irrigation, and recreation since 1955.

It was a hot fire on a cold January night in 1959 at J. C. Penney, 140 South Santa Fe Avenue. At his retirement, late fire chief Ed Bross recalled, "That was a cold bitter night. I don't think any of us thought we'd make it through the night. The temperature was below zero; ice formed where water dripped from the hydrants, icicles formed on the aerial truck. Man that was cold."

Leo Wachtel battles the elements to help push a pickup away from the curb in front of J. C. Penney around 1952. Ann's Beauty Salon and Reese Jewelry were across the street at 147 South Santa Fe Avenue and Hinkle radio service at 149 South Santa Fe Avenue. "Parking meters or not" was quite a controversy in the 1970s. The meters were finally removed around 1982.

102

This photograph was taken from Interstate 135 near Salina, looking southeast. Salina proper narrowly missed being struck by the devastating F3 tornado that caused millions of dollars in damage across north-central Kansas on September 26, 1973. This funnel cloud passed over the southeast part of town, destroying the Sundowner East mobile home park along East Magnolia Road. Roberta Ring remembers the day well. She and her husband Larry lost everything, including their trailer home, cars, and cat. That afternoon the Rings and their daughter Sherry, age 3, joined others in the trailer park's storm shelter. The noise was as loud as a train, Roberta recalls. She thought the ceiling of the shelter would collapse. From the shelter window, someone saw a horse fly by. After the storm, they had to crawl under a truck that was blocking the doorway. The Rings found their bathtub in a pasture east of the trailer park. Roberta discovered a ceramic frog lying on the ground without a chip, while the dryer it had sat upon was irreparably mangled.

Do-si-do and promenade! Dunbar School students perform at a musical festival at Memorial Hall, 410 West Ash Street, in the early 1950s. Completed in 1924, Memorial Hall was used over the years for live entertainment, church conferences, conventions, and school functions like basketball games and tournaments, graduation ceremonies, and all-school music festivals until the new community building, Bicentennial Center, was erected in 1979.

When built in 1921 at 509 East Elm Street as a school for the black community, Dunbar School was the only elementary school in Salina that had a gymnasium. Dunbar was named for poet-author Paul Laurence Dunbar, who lived from 1872 to 1906. Segregation in the public schools ended in 1954, and the school was closed by 1956. The building now houses administration offices for St. Francis Community Services, a behavioral health care organization.

By the latter 1960s, a second high school in Salina was needed to meet population needs. Salina South High School at 730 East Magnolia Road, designed by Wilson and Company and Shaver Architects, opened for classes in the fall of 1970. An open classroom concept in three circular pods proved a challenge for visitors or newcomers to the school. Salina High School (below) at 650 East Crawford Street, designed by Kansas City architect Joe Radotinsky, was built in 1951. The completion of South High School necessitated a new name for the "old" school. It became Salina Central High School. School improvements continue. A master plan was developed to convert the high schools and other facilities to state-of-the-art academic schools by replacing roofs, complying with accessibility requirements, and remodeling theaters and physical fitness areas. Central had not been air-conditioned prior to a recent face lift. (At right, courtesy of USD 305.)

Moonlight Scene at the Western Star Mill Dam, Salina, Kansas.

The Western Star Mill and dam, the oldest and only remaining mill, is now operated by ADM Milling Company. Scenes from *Picnic*, starring Kim Novak and William Holden, were shot from the Smoky Hill River area near this mill in 1955, pictured here in a romanticized moonlight view. The 1980 comedy *Up the Academy* was also filmed in Salina, mostly on the St. John Military School grounds.

Salina celebrated its centennial in a big way in 1958. The theme "Wagons to Wings" was also the title of a six-day pageant performed by a cast of 750 at the Kenwood athletic field. The festivities ended with a fireworks display. Residents have fond memories of a parade and window displays, costumes and contests, and souvenir place mats and tokens that were available at the Lamer Hotel headquarters.

106

While it has not been many years since an attendant appeared at the gas pump to fuel vehicles, it has been a while since gas was available for 18.9¢ per gallon. Cars line up at the Hudson Oil station at 622 North Santa Fe Avenue around 1956. The federal minimum wage was $1 in 1956, with an average annual income of $4,454. A postage stamp was 3¢, and an average home cost $22,000.

Remember going to dollar night at the outdoor drive-in movies with a car full of people and hanging that speaker on the car window? By the 1970s, drive-in theaters were on their way out, with only a few operating in Kansas in 2008. Gary Chrisbens was manager of the 81 Drive-In Theatre on the south edge of Salina from 1957 to 1974. Putting his skills to work, Chrisbens has been volunteer projectionist at the Salina Art Cinema at 150 South Santa Fe Avenue since the theater opened in 1997. (Courtesy of Al Mattson.)

Founded as the *Saline County Journal* in 1871, the *Salina Journal* evolved through a series of mergers and acquisitions. *Journal* staff around 1950, from left to right, include Virgil Laubengayer, composing room employee Louie Bates, press room foreman Eldon Oscar Wood, an unidentified circulation manager, Glen Williams, Earl Woodward, Peter McDonald, and editor/publisher from 1949 to 1975 Whitley Austin.

U. S. Post Office, Salina, Kansas.

This impressive building, known as the castle, was built as a federal government building, post office, and court in 1895 on the southwest corner of Seventh Street and Iron Avenue. When a new post office was built to the west of this building in 1937, the building became home for the *Salina Journal* and KSAL radio. Razed in 1966, the property is now a parking lot.

108

In 1939, Dorethea R. Smith was one of the few women city editors in the country. Born on November 4, 1893, Smith graduated from Salina High School in 1910, serving as associate editor of the school annual, and Kansas Wesleyan University, Salina. Her love of newspaper work began as a proofreader at a salary of $6 a week. She became a reporter during World War I and eventually the city editor for the *Salina Journal*. For her, newspaper work was like "living a bright dream." When she retired from the *Salina Journal* in 1956, she joined the *Salina Sun* in the society and feature department and worked as a Salina-based stringer for Kansas newspapers. On the day of her death at age 75, Smith was covering a city commission meeting as a part-time reporter for a Wichita newspaper.

The history of women's clubs in Salina goes back to the 1800s when women across the nation were organizing interest and study groups. The Kansas Federated Women's Club, later the 20th Century Club, began in 1895, dividing into districts. A subsidiary, the Sacred Literature Club, shown with 1971 club members, supported music and arts in Salina from 1914 until the 1990s. Records show that the Sacred Literature Study Club donated a Birger Sandzen painting to Salina Public Library in 1937.

Kenwood park stadium, shown beyond the bleachers in the photograph, was the finest around when the Salina Millers and Ban Johnson leagues played there in the 1930s and when the minor-league Blue Jays made Salina their home from 1946 until 1952. The area was changed to a rodeo arena in 1978, when eight ball diamonds were constructed in lower Indian Rock Park. Over the years, Salina's Bill Rogell, Bob Swift, Bob Cain, Gene Mauch, Pat Meares, and Ryan Kohlmeier went on to play major-league baseball.

Tony's Little Italy opened about 1957 as a cozy little restaurant specializing in pizza, a new food that quickly became the rage. Gregory "Tony" Paglia started the eatery, located at 244A South Santa Fe Avenue, and operated it for several years. Part of his business was selling half-baked frozen pizzas to taverns. Paglia's brother-in-law Dick Barlow acquired the restaurant and pizza-making business in 1963. About 1969, he expanded the frozen pizza line into a manufacturing building at the Airport Industrial Center on the former military base property at Schilling and Centennial Roads. The factory opened with a dozen workers. In 1970, Schwan's Food Company bought Tony's Pizza from Barlow. Today the company provides retail frozen pizzas as well as other food intended for school cafeterias and institutions. It is Salina's largest employer with around 2,000 employees.

244 South Santa Fe

TO OUR GUESTS

Satisfying you, the public, is our desire, to give you the pleasures of eating . . . The custom and habits of home, is our set policy of excellent home style Italian cooking, which you find to your taste. Let us suggest or serve you any of our specialties on which we so proudly base our reputation.

### PIZZA

| | Small | Medium | Large |
|---|---|---|---|
| Cheese | .75 | 1.00 | 1.75 |
| Onion | .85 | 1.35 | 2.35 |
| Tomato | .85 | 1.35 | 2.35 |
| Green Pepper | .85 | 1.35 | 2.35 |
| Garlic | .85 | 1.35 | 2.35 |
| Sausage | .85 | 1.35 | 2.35 |
| Hamburger | .85 | 1.35 | 2.35 |
| Anchovy | 1.00 | 1.50 | 2.50 |
| Bacon | .85 | 1.35 | 2.35 |
| Pepperoni | 1.00 | 1.50 | 2.50 |
| Mushroom | 1.00 | 1.50 | 2.50 |
| Tuna Fish | 1.00 | 1.50 | 2.50 |
| Bar-S Ham | 1.25 | 1.75 | 2.75 |
| Shrimp | 1.25 | 1.75 | 2.75 |
| Salami | 1.25 | 1.75 | 2.75 |
| Deluxe | 2.00 | 3.00 | 4.00 |

15c extra for each combination added on small; 25c on medium; 35c on large.

### APPETIZERS

| | |
|---|---|
| Italian Antipasto | 1.00 |
| Provolone Cheese | .40 |
| Anchovies, Filets | .40 |
| Italian Salami | .40 |
| Italian Capacollo | .40 |
| Celery and Olives | .50 |
| Pickled Peppers (Hot or Sweet) | .30 |
| Shrimp Cocktail | .65 |
| Tomato Juice | .20 |
| Orange Juice | .20 |

### FAMOUS ITALIAN DINNER
(SERVES TWO)

Soup
Braciole
With Choice of Mostaccioli or Spaghetti
Italian Salad Bowl
Garlic Bread
Dessert
Served with Small Cheese, Sausage,
or Hamburger Pizza
Serving for Two $4.95

★ ★

### SPECIAL DINNERS

These are Familiar Italian Foods—Prepared and Served by Tony's Famous Recipes.

LASAGNA (Our Most Famous Dish) layers of noodles, interlaced with cheese and meat, baked, and served with our famous meat sauce . . . . . 1.75

BRACIOLE, Rolled Beef Steak, stuffed with our own special ingredients, cooked and served with our famous sauce . . . . . . . . . . 1.75

RAVIOLI — Meat . . . . . . . . . 1.65
Made with Chicken, Beef and Pork

GNOCHI, Specially made, potato, noodle, made daily, served with our famous sauce . . . . . . . . 1.75

FRIED PEPPERS AND EGGS . . . . . 1.35
Above served with choice of juice, cocktail, salad, garlic bread, drink, dessert.

May We Suggest Our Delicious
GARLIC BREAD
15c Per Order

NOT RESPONSIBLE FOR

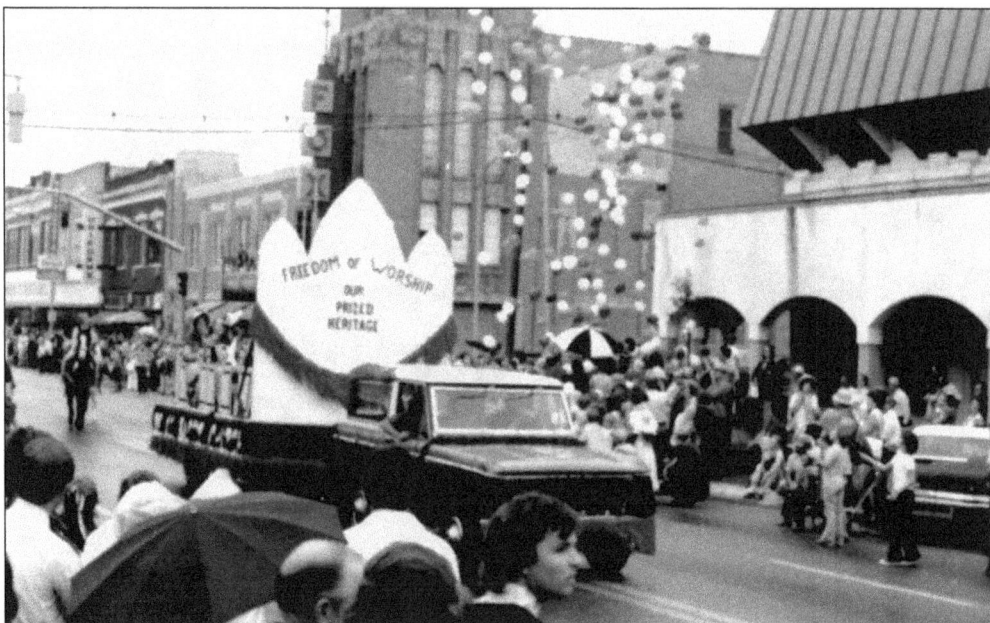

Threatening showers delayed the 1976 Happy Birthday America parade but could not dampen the large crowd's enthusiasm. Free watermelon, fire hydrant painting contests, Silver Sabers drum and bugle corps, block parties, a street fair, and a fireworks display at the airport provided a spirit of unity for the homegrown celebration. Projects of a lasting nature brought Salina much splendor: a needlepoint mural hanging in the City-County Building; an outdoor environmental lab; *Trifinity* sculpture; Bicentennial Center; and Founders Park with a time capsule.

The gazebo was built as an entertainment stage for the 1976 downtown street fair, which paved the way for the annual Smoky Hill River Festival. After the street fair, the gazebo was moved to Oakdale Park, where it stayed for nearly 20 years. When a new stage was built in Oakdale, the gazebo was moved to Jerry Ivey Park at the southwest corner of Ohio Street and Magnolia Road, where it continues to be used for entertainment and an occasional wedding.

*Six*

# ALL-AMERICA CITY
## 1980–2008

Billed as the "Highway to Heaven," downtown Salina enthusiastically welcomed the Great American Race participants on June 26, 1991. Fifteen thousand spectators, billowy clouds, heaven's gates, a setting sun, dancers, a colorful rainbow, lively Swedish dancers, clowns, and the Salina Municipal Band greeted the antique automobile rally drivers and navigators. Participants voted Salina as the rally's Great American City and awarded a $5,000 prize to the Salina Public Library. (Photography by Tom Dorsey; courtesy of the Salina Journal.)

Wes Jackson (right), president of the Land Institute and a plant geneticist, is examining locally grown Indian grass with Jerry Glover, a soil scientist. Founded in 1976, the institute was designed to explore methods for creating a sustainable agriculture, with less waste, by using little or no chemicals and irrigation and planting perennial crops that would produce year after year. A Kansas native and farmer, Jackson sees his work as "simply an extension of love," helping the future world's soil to produce enough food to sustain possibly 10 billion people. (Photograph by Jim Richardson; courtesy of the Land Institute.)

The Tammy Walker Cancer Center at 511 South Santa Fe Avenue provides comprehensive cancer care and convenience for those battling the disease. In 2004, the Walker Family Foundation donated a gift of $500,000 for the center's fund-raising campaign in memory of Tammy Walker, who died from lung cancer at the age of 11. A bronze sculpture, *Running Free*, depicts a happy child and was later placed in front of the center.

114

"Play ball!" can be heard most summer evenings at the Dean Evans Stadium, located at the East Crawford Recreation Area. Dean Evans was a supporter of youth baseball and a member of the Kansas Sports Hall of Fame, and founded Evans Grain Company. Many Salina citizens fondly remember the beautiful Christmas light display at his Highland Avenue home. Evans left his mark on Salina in a quiet, selfless manner. He died in 1991.

**DEAN EVANS**

A Grateful City Remembers

For over half a century, S. Dean Evans, Sr., helped Salina grow and prosper. philanthropy helped make Salina a better place to live. His commitment to h Salina's youth and his support of youth baseball have made Salina a great pl play ball. This stadium was erected in his honor by the City of Salina and th private contributions to Salina Baseball Enterprises, Inc. A grateful city reme Dean's civic legacy and thanks those individuals and organizations named Together with many other contributors, they have all carried on the tradi community service Dean embodied by giving their time and resources to b Dean Evans Stadium

Dedicated
30 July 1992

The pillars from the former YMCA building (1910–1978) located at 315 West Iron Avenue are reminders of the rich history the organization has experienced in providing a place in Salina for fitness and health. The current YMCA building located at 570 YMCA Drive was dedicated in 1978. It is one of the best in the country for offering a variety of activities for its members, including an indoor swimming pool, handball-racquetball courts, and weight rooms.

"Salina looks like a tiny dot," stated Salina's own, astronaut, astrophysicist, and NASA administrator Steve Hawley to a group of children in 1997 about what he saw from the space shuttle. From 1986 to 1999, he was involved with five space shuttle missions. He was instrumental in taking to space the Hubble Space Telescope, whose pictures fascinated the world.

Aiming for the former Schilling Air Force Base flight line, the Virgin Atlantic GlobalFlyer, flown by Steve Fossett, was making flight history. After 67 hours, 2 minutes, 38 seconds, and 23,000 miles, the GlobalFlyer arrived home, after circling the globe without refueling, safe and sound. This once-in-a-lifetime event definitely put Salina on the global map as every aspect of the flight was reviewed by people worldwide via the Internet, television, and radio. (Photograph by Jeff Cooper; courtesy of the Salina Journal.)

The first woman mayor, elected in 1979, Karen Graves will long be remembered for her tireless work within the Salina community. She engineered the Goals for Salina project that helped to garner the All-America Award in 1989, helped secure the bond funding for the Bicentennial Center construction, and was active in the Salina Arts and Humanities Commission. Graves moved to St. Joseph, Missouri, in 1992. (Photograph by Tom Dorsey; courtesy of the Salina Journal.)

"Every minute of every day, I think about music," said Eric Stein. Moving to Salina in 1951, he worked as the music teacher at Sacred Heart High School and was the organist and choir director for Sacred Heart Cathedral. He was the founder of the Salina Symphony and Salina Youth Symphony and directed the Salina Municipal Band. As a musician, educator, and conductor, he touched the cultural life of Salina until his death in 2007.

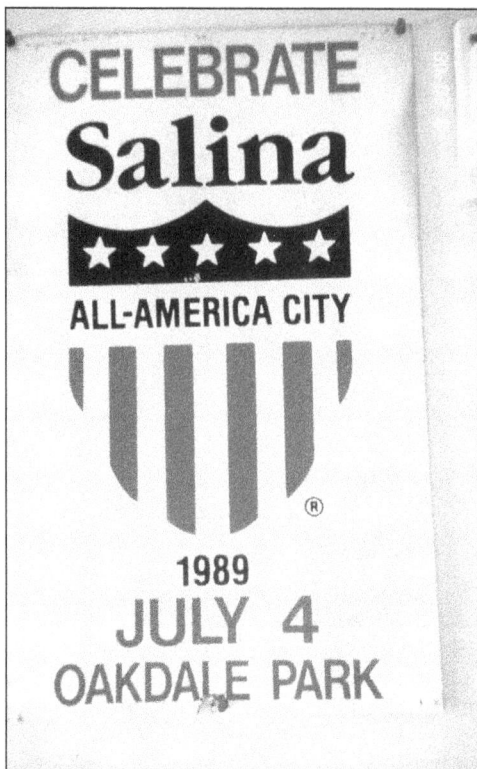

On May 13, 1989, the National Civic League pronounced Salina (with a long I) as one of the top 10 All-America cities. The judges especially liked the Goals for Salina project in which 300 volunteers studied the city and made recommendations. When Salina received the All-America City award on July 4, over 4,000 gathered in Oakdale Park to celebrate. Children dressed up like Uncle Sam in the 94-degree heat, while hot dogs sizzled on the grill.

The "River Rascals," directed by Colleen Jewel and accompanied by Martha Suttle, added a patriotic flavor to the July 4, 1989, festivities at Oakdale Park. Nine "Rascal Editions," from 1987 to 1995, provided children in grades four through eight with a great musical opportunity. "They came to us with everything they needed; we provided the music and 'shaping,'" stated Jewel. Here they perform the "Goals for Salina March."

In 1922, hamburger and onion met a grill, and the one-of-a-kind Cozy burger was created. The Cozy Inn still operates in the same small white building at 108 North Seventh Street. The burgers have been noted in magazines and are shipped across the world to aficionados. The Cozy Inn celebrates its 86th anniversary in 2008 and reminds one of a time when a nickel could buy the best burger in town.

Luong Van Te and his family are pictured at home in Salina, a long way from Vietnam and the hardships experienced in the 1970s. The first Vietnamese refugees arrived in Salina in 1975. By 1979, most of the 300 Southeast Asian refugees had arrived. They struggled with learning English and understanding American culture, customs, and laws. The Indochinese Resettlement Program, located at 410 West Iron Avenue, provided education and emotional assistance to the immigrants.

In October 1993, William P. Graves, Salina native, chose his hometown in which to announce his candidacy for governor of Kansas. His bid for election was successful, and at the age of 41, he became one of the youngest governors in Kansas history. He won reelection in 1998 with 74 percent of the vote. A 1976 graduate of Kansas Wesleyan University, Salina, Graves also served as Kansas secretary of state from 1986 to 1994. (Photograph by Tom Dorsey; courtesy of the Salina Journal.)

At nine feet tall and weighing two tons, the *Trifinity* bronze sculpture graces the area between the City-County Building and the Salina Public Library. Representing the three phases of time—past, present, and future—Salina artist Dr. Richard Bergen designed the sculpture to demonstrate the flow of time and movement. The January 30, 1975, dedication was one of the first events celebrating America's bicentennial in 1976.

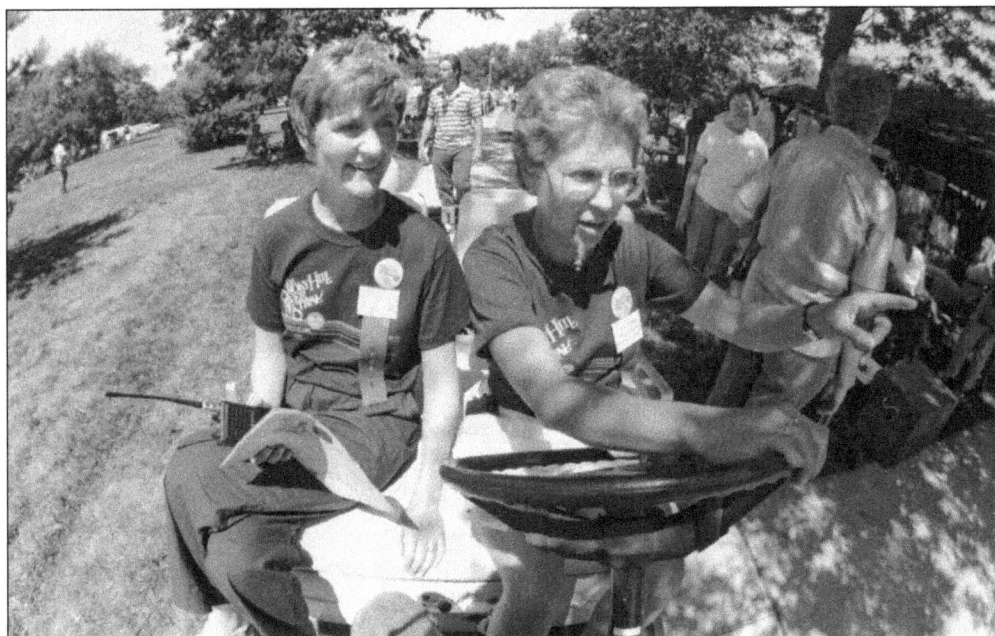

From its birth in 1977, the Smoky Hill River Festival has been a popular summer event. Martha Rhea (left), and Lana Jordan, festival coordinator, are busy with the details required to make a festival happen. Rhea, Arts and Humanities Commission director, stated in 1977, "The Festival will put Salina on the map." And indeed it has, growing and evolving over the years. (Courtesy of the Salina Journal.)

"Where's the grass?" This lively relay was part of the 1989 Santa Fe Day festivities, held annually in September. Entertainment, arts and crafts booths, food vendors, games, and a parade celebrated the community's heritage in downtown Salina. In 2007, the Smoky Hill Museum took over organization of the event, renaming it the Street Fair. In the background the six-story, neoclassic Masonic temple, completed in 1927, occupies a prominent place at 336 South Santa Fe Avenue. (Photograph by Scott Williams; courtesy of the Salina Journal.)

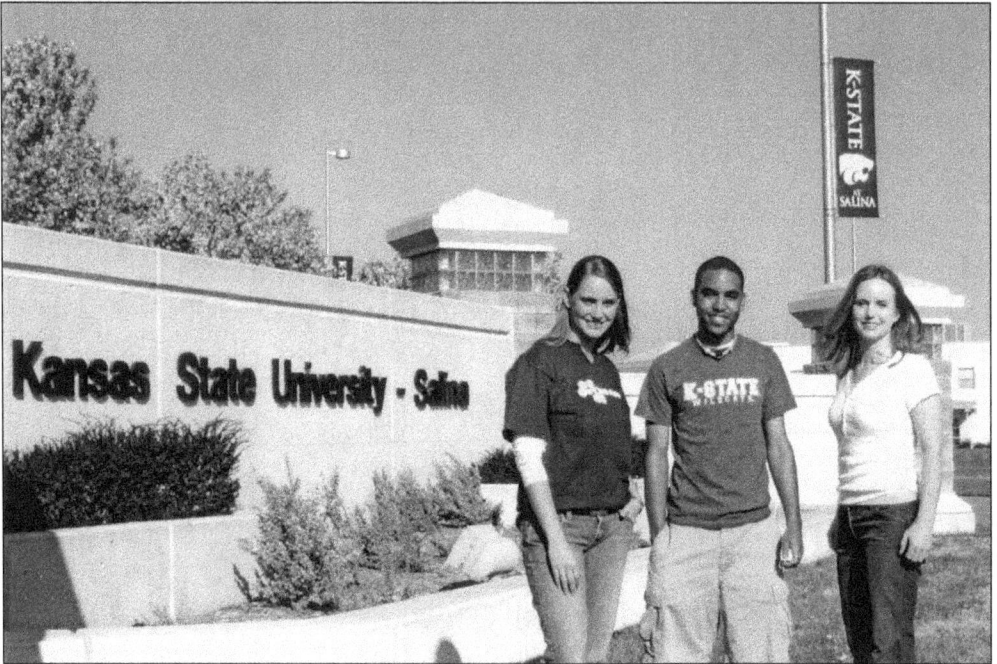

Kansas State University, Salina, is a blend of technology and higher education. In 1965, the first Kansas technology college, Schilling Institute, began classes. In 1968, the institute was changed to Kansas Technical Institute (KTI). In 1988, KTI was changed to Kansas College of Technology (KCT), providing a two-year study in the fields of science and engineering. In 1991, KCT merged with Kansas State University. Pictured from left to right are students Lindsey Dreiling, Brian Dorsey, and Carol Dawson. (Courtesy of Kansas State University-Salina.)

Salina Christian Academy, "putting Christ at the heart of education," opened in 2003 with 70 children at 1325 East Cloud Street, home of the former Emmanuel Christian School. In the fall of 2004, Salina Christian Academy moved its school to the former Lowell Elementary School (above) at 1009 Highland Avenue. The addition of middle school grades occurred in the fall of 2006, and as the school looks to the future, one goal is the addition of a high school.

A Salina legend and trailblazer, Robert Chester Caldwell (1913–1999) was honored in 2000 with the dedication of the Robert Caldwell Plaza, located between the City-County Building and Salina Public Library. Here Caldwell is standing near Dunbar School, where he began his career in education. His many accomplishments include Salina and Kansas Teacher of the Year, Salina city commissioner, Salina's first African American mayor, and the Kansas House of Representatives, to name a few. (Photograph by Tom Dorsey; courtesy of the Salina Journal.)

Cottonwood Elementary School, located near the intersection of Walnut Street and Phillips Avenue, opened for classes in the fall of 2002. Cottonwood and Lakewood Middle School were the two new facilities built as part of a multimillion-dollar bond project approved by Salina voters in 1998. Existing schools were updated to meet the needs of a new century, including technology, computers, air-conditioning, larger media centers, a centralized school office, and efficient handicapped-accessible buildings.

Salina native Tyrees Allen (right) performs here with Heather Roberts in the October 2002 production of *Othello* at the Salina Community Theatre. Allen has appeared on stage, film, television, and Broadway. A 1972 graduate of Salina Central High School and graduate of Marymount College, Allen has appeared in several other local productions. He can currently be seen in the *Women's Murder Club* television series. (Courtesy of the Salina Community Theatre.)

George Murdock, known in Salina as George Sawaya Jr., portrays Henry Drummond in the 2001 Salina Community Theatre's presentation of *Inherit the Wind*. The actors on stage are, from left to right, Jack Stewart, Murdock, and Royce Tinkler. Because of his strong features, Murdock usually plays the "heavy" on stage, film, and television. The veteran actor has played character roles on television shows including *Bonanza*, *Barney Miller*, *The Untouchables*, *Gunsmoke*, *L.A. Law*, and *Night Court*. (Courtesy of the Salina Community Theatre.)

Michael Henry, the first director of Salina Community Access Television, came to Salina in 1992 from California to start a volunteer community cable television operation. It was formally established on April 4, 1992. Henry also oversaw the renovation of Memorial Hall at 410 West Ash Street into a television studio. The occasion in this photograph, taken May 28, 1993, is the "Premier Party", an invitation-only gathering to celebrate the first live telecast from the newly completed television studio. (Photograph by Tom Dorsey; courtesy of the Salina Journal.)

The curtain went up on this building on June 14, 1973, with grand opening ceremonies that included a visit from then governor Robert Docking and the staging of *The Music Man*. Originating from a 1950s theater group named the Curtain Callers, the Salina Community Theatre formed as a nonprofit organization in 1960, holding productions wherever it could—Oakdale Park, a barn in Indian Rock Park, or more often in the old Washington High School. (Courtesy of Salina Community Theatre.)

Salina Regional Hospital Center on South Santa Fe Avenue benefits from its location in a crossroads city, enabling it to be a medical hub for the region. Far removed from the limited facility and equipment of its 1920s beginning, the center's services now include cardiac services, surgical care, physical and respiratory therapy, mental health, infant stimulation, home health, and sleep disorder treatment. The new six-story bed tower at the Santa Fe campus will soon be completed. (Courtesy of Salina Regional Health Center.)

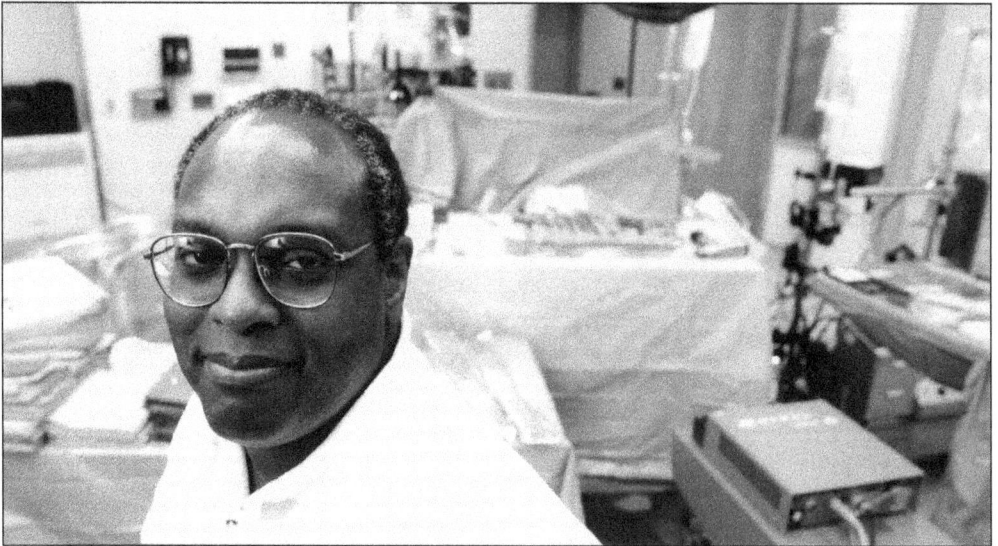

Dr. Maceo "Mace" Braxton Jr. pioneered the heart surgery program and served as a cardiothoracic surgeon at the Salina Regional Health Center from 1998 until his death on February 15, 2008. Born on April 7, 1953, in Los Angeles, California, he went on to graduate from West Point in 1974. Braxton retired from the U.S. Army in 1998 as a lieutenant colonel. He will be remembered as a compassionate and accomplished man. (Photograph by Marc Hall; courtesy of the Salina Journal.)

The Salina Public Library has evolved from "reading rooms" of the 1890s to a Carnegie-funded building completed in 1903, and finally to a facility today that meets the diverse needs of the community. In 1968, the library moved to the building shown here at 301 West Elm Street. Renovation projects completed in 1996 and 2007 have expanded the building and increased services. A separate additional space called the Community Learning Center was opened in 2008.

After months of planning and work, the Smoky Hill Museum celebrated its grand opening in October 1986. The renovated post office building at 211 West Iron Avenue held the historical collection of artifacts started by Alexander M. Campbell Jr. Prior to its move, the museum was housed first at the Carnegie Public Library and then in the Oakdale Park bathhouse. In this photograph the Smoky Hill Museum salutes the city for its 150 years. Happy Birthday, Salina!

Visit us at
arcadiapublishing.com

www.ingramcontent.com/pod-product-compliance
Lightning Source LLC
Chambersburg PA
CBHW050659150426
42813CB00055B/2295